**EMOTION REGULATION CONSUMPTION:
EXAMINING THE EFFECTS OF EMOTIONS AND SELF-REGULATION ON
CONSUMPTION BEHAVIOR**

EMOTION REGULATION CONSUMPTION: EXAMINING THE EFFECTS OF EMOTIONS AND SELF-REGULATION ON CONSUMPTION BEHAVIOR

A dissertation submitted in partial
fulfillment of the requirements for the degree of
Doctorate of Philosophy

By

Elyria Kemp, B.S, M.B.A
Bradley University, 1995
University of New Orleans, 2003

May 2008
University of Arkansas

UMI Number: 3317822

INFORMATION TO USERS

The quality of this reproduction is dependent upon the quality of the copy submitted. Broken or indistinct print, colored or poor quality illustrations and photographs, print bleed-through, substandard margins, and improper alignment can adversely affect reproduction.

In the unlikely event that the author did not send a complete manuscript and there are missing pages, these will be noted. Also, if unauthorized copyright material had to be removed, a note will indicate the deletion.

ABSTRACT

Research has demonstrated that positive emotions such as joy, contentment and interest can help in facilitating coping behavior and reducing defensiveness when individuals must deal with adverse events and situations. Positive emotions can help to regulate negative emotions by "undoing" the psychological or cognitive narrowing engendered by negative emotions. This research explored how, why and under what circumstances consumers purchase products in an effort to "down-regulate" or decrease negative emotions. Different forms of consumption may be used as a coping response to mitigate negative emotions. Specifically, individuals may purchase hedonic products to help regulate emotions because these products can facilitate and perpetuate feelings of enjoyment. This research examined a phenomenon known as Emotion Regulation Consumption (ERC). Emotion regulation consumption in this research refers specifically to the consumption or purchase of a good or service for the purposes of alleviating, repairing, or managing an affective state. This phenomenon was examined with respect to the "broaden-and-build" theory of positive emotions (Fredrickson 1998, 2001) as well as resource-based approaches to self-regulation and mood (Aspinwall 1998; Baumeister et al. 1998). Additionally, differences in the way that individuals cognitively exercise control over their emotions, or an emotion regulation strategy known as cognitive reappraisal (Gross and John 2003), was examined for its moderating role in ERC.

The ERC phenomenon was examined in this research using four discrete emotions (amusement, contentment, sadness and fear/anxiety). Three complete studies were conducted to test hypotheses. The first study examined the effect of emotions on the consumption of hedonic goods as well as tested for the moderating role of cognitive reappraisal. The second study examined the effect of emotions, self-regulation, and cognitive reappraisal on impulse control. Finally, the third study assessed actual behavior with regard to ERC by having subjects engage in a choice/decision task.

Findings from this research provide evidence that ERC is a phenomenon enlisted by the typical consumer. Studying ERC may lead to greater enlightenment regarding the effect that pre-existing emotions have on consumption behavior.

ACKNOWLEDGEMENTS

As I purposefully make an effort to do regarding every achievement in my life, I give thanks to Jehovah God, who has been my protector, provider and comforter. Without Him nothing would be possible for me, but with Him, everything is possible.

I would also like to acknowledge my family. My siblings and my very special nephew, Theodore, have been a tremendous source of encouragement, sanity and support to me. Very importantly, I would like to thank the people responsible for bringing me into this world, my parents—Eramus and Eva Kemp. Even though my father, Eramus, is not here to physically witness my accomplishments, his spirit and character reside with me. My mother, Eva, unrelenting in her dedication and support, is worthy of this degree conferred upon me, ten times over.

In addition to my family, I am honored to have such wonderful friends. I would like to give special thanks to Pat Edwards, who has convinced me that angelic-like qualities can manifest themselves in people on earth. I am also very grateful to have such uplifting and faithful individuals in my life such as Barbara Lofton, Terry Esper, Joanna Newman, Donna Daniels, my PhD Project buddies and My Bui. My old lunch buddies—Kim, Julie, Maureen and Angela—have, and still prove to be one of my greatest support systems and to them I am forever thankful.

I would also like to express much gratitude towards the people that have made my tenure here at Arkansas a fruitful one, including my committee members, Scot Burton, Betsy Howlett and Jeff Murray. From these bright individuals, I have received solid training. Also, much thanks to all those on faculty and staff— Dub Ashton, Molly Jensen, Nicole Cox, John Cole, Dr. Kurtz, Bob Stassen, my officemates, the guys in the

Tech Center, Claudia Mobley, Don Bland, the administrative assistants, student workers—and the Department's fearless leader, Tom Jensen.

Last, but certainly not least, I would like to thank the individual for whom I have the utmost respect. His *patience*, support, encouragement, instruction, wisdom and humor have not only helped me succeed in this endeavor, but over the course of the past four years I have had the opportunity to witness an exceptional scholar and mentor in action. I am truly grateful to Steven W. Kopp. He embodies so many of the qualities that scholarly mentors should possess. I hope that one-day modern science will be able to clone professors like him.

DEDICATION

This dissertation is dedicated to my mother, Eva Mae Kemp, and her coffee table.

Thanks for always believing in me.

TABLE OF CONTENTS

CHAPTER 1

Introduction and Overview

INTRODUCTION

Marketers have long made attempts to encourage individuals to use consumption as a way to manage, or regulate, their emotions. This is evidenced by advertising appeals that have become embedded in our culture—"You deserve a break today" (McDonald's), "For all you do, this Bud's for you," (Budweiser) and "Celebrate the moments of your life" (General Foods International Coffee). Conventional wisdom suggests that people would rather feel good than bad. Such hedonic tendencies have also been implied in the behavioral literatures, proposing that people experiencing negative emotions may make conscious efforts to "down-regulate" negative affective states (Baumeister 2002; Fredrickson 2000; Gross, Richards and John 2006; Mayne 2001). Although consumer researchers have acknowledged the role that affect, mood and emotions play in judgment, choice and behavior (Bagozzi and Moore 1994; Burke and Edell 1989; Pham 1998; Louro, Pieters and Zeelenberg 2005; Moore, Harris and Chen 1995; Raghunathan and Pham 1999), few studies exist in the literature that have explored how consumers might use consumption to regulate affective states in everyday life. This research explores the role that discrete emotions play in the consumption process by examining how consumers might use consumption as a mechanism for regulating, or managing, their emotions.

EMOTION REGULATION CONSUMPTION

Emotion regulation consumption (ERC) in this research refers specifically to the consumption or purchase of a good or service for the purposes of alleviating, repairing, or managing an affective state. This research suggests that emotion regulation consumption is a prosaic occurrence in the lives of individuals and central to well being. For example, a countless number of individuals wake themselves with a cup of coffee in

2

the morning; some treat themselves to a nice dinner for a job well-done; others may purchase goods of either intrinsic or extrinsic (e.g. jewelry, cars) value to make themselves feel better (Mick and DeMoss 1990).

Research has provided evidence that the most commonly regulated affective states are negative ones (Gross, John and Richards 2006; Lazarus 1991; Morris and Reilly 1987). Thayer (1996) examined what activities individuals engaged in to deal with, or regulate, negative emotions. They found that a common mechanism employed for managing negative emotions, with 51% of respondents reporting using this method, was engaging in positive social interaction. Exercising cognitive control (changing negative thoughts) was also a popular emotion regulation technique (51%). Other behaviors respondents reported using to change negative affective states included listening to music (47%), eating (34%), watching television (25%), and going shopping (25%). As evidenced by the work of Thayer (1996), some form of consumption—whether it be shopping or eating—may be used as a way to infuse positive emotions into one's life. Subsequently, emotion regulation consumption is a phenomenon acknowledged and enlisted by the typical consumer.

However, emotion regulation consumption may have a dark side. Individuals may choose to regulate or manage emotions by engaging in aversive health-affecting behavior such as excessive drinking, over-eating, illicit drugs or promiscuous sexual behavior. These consumption activities may develop into compulsive and addictive behaviors (Davison and Neale 1986; Elliot 1994; Hirschman 1992; Hoch and Loewenstein 1991). Today, over 40 million American adults battle alcohol or drug addiction (Rubin 2006). Many of these addictions and compulsive behaviors started because of the positive reinforcement received by the individuals immediately after performing such behaviors. After continuous reinforcement, these behaviors became habits. Each time the behavior was reinforced, the habit was strengthened (Thayer 1996; Hirschman 1992). Eventually, exercising self-control over the desire to perform the behavior (Hoch and Loewenstein 1991) became impossible.

Another pernicious result of emotion regulation consumption may involve impulsive and excessive shopping or spending. More than half of Americans struggle to control excessive spending and debt (Perry 2002). In particular, credit cards have become lifestyle facilitators for many, whose use may be spurred by a need to self-medicate and gratify (Bernthal, Crockett and Rose 2005). In fact, impulse buying accounts for 64% of supermarket sales (Abrahams 1997; Smith 1996) and the purchase of new products result more from impulse rather than prior planning (Sfiligoj 1996). Research suggests that impulse spending may be hedonically motivated. Rook (1987) found that 41% of respondents said that impulse buying made them feel good, happy and satisfied. Those feeling down said that it made them feel better. Others said impulse buying afforded them an opportunity to indulge in a special treat or reward.

In the research that follows, emotion regulation consumption was examined by studying what effects discrete emotions such as amusement, sadness, contentment and fear/anxiety have on consumption behavior. This is somewhat of a departure from previous research in the consumer behavioral literatures on emotion regulation and management. Much of the research to date has examined primarily global affective states (positive affect versus negative affect or good moods versus bad moods) in exploring this phenomenon (Faber and Christensen 1996; Mick and DeMoss 1990).

4

Studying specific emotions with regard to emotion regulation has special implications for consumer research. Research by emotion theorists has provided evidence that different emotions (even of the same valence) result in different appraisals of the environment and action tendencies (Frijda 1986; Lazarus 1984, 1991 Smith and Ellsworth 1985). As part of the preliminary research for the studies to follow, a classroom of college students was asked about how their consumption differed based on the specific emotion they were experiencing. Individuals were asked what they might purchase to make themselves feel better when they were angry, sad, happy and proud. When feeling angry or sad, most students reported that they would be inclined to consume alcohol or high carbohydrate-content foods. However, when feeling happy or joyful, many indicated that they would want engage in some type of social interaction with friends. When feeling proud, many reported buying a new garment or buying something special to add to a collection. Subsequently, individuals may engage in different types of consumption based on the emotion experienced.

This research sought to explain why, how and under what circumstances emotion regulation consumption might occur. Specifically, it examined whether people that were experiencing negative emotions (sadness, fear/anxiety) were more likely to engage in forms of consumption, particularly of a hedonic nature, to regulate their emotions than those experiencing positive emotions (amusement, contentment).

Additionally, coping with negative affect may lead to poor self-regulation (Muraven and Baumeister 2000). When people are experiencing negative emotion, the goal of feeling better often exercises primacy over self-control. People may eat unhealthy foods, procrastinate, seek immediate gratification and even engage in

5

impulsive behavior (Muraven and Baumeister 2000; Baumeister 2002; Tice, Bratslavsky and Baumeister 2001). This research also examined whether individuals whose psychological resources had been depleted were more likely to engage in impulsive consumption.

Research from the psychology literature suggests that individuals can cognitively exercise control over their emotions by using strategies to influence how and when they experience certain emotions (Lazarus and Alfert 1964). One common emotion regulation strategy is cognitive reappraisal (Gross and John 1998). This research also examined whether individual differences in the way that people manage their emotions has an effect on consumption behavior. ERC may be contingent on an individual's proclivity to employ such a cognitive emotion regulation strategy.

OVERVIEW OF CONCEPTUAL FRAMEWORK

The following research was predicated on a conceptual framework using the broaden-and-build theory of positive emotions (Fredrickson 1998, 2000, 20001) along with resource-based approaches to self-regulation and mood (Aspinwall 1998, 2005; Baumeister, Bratslavsky, Muraven and Tice 1998; Tice, Bratslavsky and Baumeister 2001). In addition, this research introduced a construct to the consumer research literature regarding emotion regulation known as cognitive reappraisal (Gross and John 2003).

Broaden-and-Build Theory of Positive Emotions

The broaden-and-build theory of positive emotions (Fredrickson 1998, 2000, 2001) proposes that positive emotions such as joy, interest, and love have the ability to broaden thought-action repertoire and build psychological, social, intellectual and

6

physical resources. Specifically related to emotion regulation, the broaden-and-build theory proposes that positive emotions have the ability to "undo" or "down-regulate" the effect of negative emotions.

Studies from the consumer research literature have demonstrated that individuals may engage in purchase or consumption behavior to down-regulate or decrease negative emotions felt (Garg, Wansink, Inman 2007; Andrade 2005; Elliot 1994; Mick amd DeMoss 1990; Faber and Christenson 1996; Mano 1999). These individuals may be making efforts to experience positive emotions by consuming products from which they derive some hedonic benefit.

Resource-Based Approaches to Self-Regulation and Mood

There may be various circumstances and conditions under which emotion regulation consumption might be more likely to occur. These circumstances may be related to an individual's available psychological resources as well as his or her ability to exercise self-regulation. Controlling one's own behavior requires the expenditure of an inner limited resource that can be reduced with use (Vohs 2005). When various demands deplete these resources, individuals may fail at self-regulation (Muraven and Baumeister 2000).

Baumeister *et al.* (1998) refer to the depletion of resources as ego depletion. Ego depletion describes the condition whereby, the self's resources are expended and the self is temporarily operating at less than full capacity. Resisting temptation and regulating emotions can deplete the self's resources. Additionally, coping with negative affect may lead to poor self-regulation (Muraven and Baumeister 2000).

7

Positive emotions may affect self-regulation by influencing a person's immediate psychological resources (Aspinwall 1998; Trope and Neter 1994). Individuals that possess a reserve of positive emotions may be more likely to maintain self-control and resist temptation (Tice, Baumeister, Shimeli and Muraven 2006). Aspinwall's (1998, 2005) resource-based approach to self-regulation predicts that if self-regard, positive emotions or subjective well-being is enjoyed above some threshold, a hedonic surplus exists. However, if self-worth and subjective well-being have been denigrated so that they fall below a certain threshold, a hedonic deficit may be experienced, and these individuals may be more likely to engage in affect repair. Applying self-regulation and the mood-as-a-resource framework in a consumption context, individuals with a reserve of positive emotions may be less likely to engage in certain forms of consumption to achieve gratification in the short-term than individuals experiencing negative emotion.

Furthermore, when an individual's psychological resources have been depleted through emotional distress, they may fail to exercise self-regulation and, thus, be more likely to engage in hedonic consumption to help restore depleted resources. A breakdown in self-regulation may also result in consumption behavior that is impulsive and possibly, excessive (Pechmann, Levine, Loughlin, and Leslie 2005).

Emotion Regulation Strategy

Individual differences in the way that people regulate their emotions may affect their consumption behavior. Research from the behavioral literatures suggests that individuals can cognitively exercise control over their emotions by using strategies to influence which emotions they experience and when they have them (Lazarus and Alfert

1964).   One common emotion regulation strategy that was used in this research was cognitive reappraisal (Gross and John 1998).

Cognitive reappraisal involves construing a potentially emotion-eliciting situation in a way that changes its emotional impact (Lazarus and Alfert 1964).   Cognitive reappraisal can alter an individual's entire emotion trajectory.   When used to down-regulate emotion, it reduces the behavioral consequences of negative emotion.   Research has found that individuals engaging in cognitive reappraisal experience and express more (in magnitude) positive emotions (Gross and John 2003).   Hence, emotion regulation consumption may be partly affected by an individual's proclivity to employ such a strategy to alter emotions.

OVERVIEW OF METHODOLOGY

Three between-subjects experiments were used to test stated hypotheses.   In all three experiments, emotions were induced via film clips.   Emotion regulation strategy (cognitive reappraisal) was measured to examine the individual effect of these factors, as well as interactive effects.   In Studies 2 and 3, an additional manipulation, ego depletion, was introduced.   Multivariate analysis of variance was performed to test the effects of these factors on dependent variables.

CONTRIBUTIONS

Theoretical Contributions

The research that follows helps to explicate why, how, and under what circumstances people might engage in consumption activities to regulate or manage emotions in everyday life. Research has demonstrated that the most commonly regulated emotions are negative emotions (Gross, Richards, John 2006; Isen 1984).   The broaden-and-build theory proposes that positive emotions undo the effects of negative emotions and act as restorers to psychological resources. People may consume products of a hedonic nature to "down-regulate" negative emotions and infuse positive emotions into their lives. Further, emotion regulation consumption may be contingent on an available supply of psychological resources. When individual's resources have been depleted, exercising self-control might become very difficult (Baumeister, Bratslavsky, Muraven and Tice 1998). According to the mood-as-resource hypothesis, people who enjoy a certain level of subjective well-being and experience positive emotions frequently, may possess a *hedonic surplus* of resources and be less likely to engage in ERC. Conversely, people who do not enjoy a certain level of subjective well-being and experience positive emotions less frequently, may be operating at a *hedonic deficit* and, thus, more likely to engage in ERC (Aspinwall 1998). Similarly, ERC may also be more likely to occur in individuals whose psychological resources have been temporarily depleted (Baumeister *et al.* 1998; Baumeister 2002)

Individual differences in the way individuals cognitively regulate their emotions may also have some impact on consumption behavior. One common emotion regulation strategy, cognitive reappraisal, involves construing a potentially emotion-eliciting situation in a way that changes its emotional impact. This emotion regulation strategy may interact with emotions to effect consumption behavior.

This research also examined ERC by focusing on the study of discrete emotions. Much of the consumer research literature has characterized affective states along a two dimensions—good versus bad or positive versus negative. However, different emotions (ie. fear, sadness, amusement, contentment) can result in different appraisals of the

10

environment (Lazarus 1984, 1994; Smith and Ellsworth 1985) and invoke different action tendencies. Research has already found that specific emotions have different impacts on judgment and choice (Lerner and Keltner 2000; Raghunathan and Corfin 2004). Hence, examining the effects of specific emotions may yield potentially different behavioral consequences for each emotion.

Substantive Contributions

Studying emotion regulation consumption has special implications for marketing. Knowing the effect that pre-existing emotions have on people can help in shaping the retail environment. For example, individuals experiencing negative emotions may be more prone to impulsive purchasing behavior. Therefore, marketers might strategically consider the placement of characteristically hedonic products in the store environment. Additionally, understanding consumer emotions and interpersonal processes can help in planning and integrating effective sales person responses to consumers (Menon and Dube 2000; Mick Demoss and Faber 1992).

Further, employing insight gleaned from the emotion regulation consumption phenomenon, marketers can better design and develop effective marketing communications for hedonic products. Creative promotions might be implemented. For example, feel-bad products (e.g. cough syrup) might be cross-promoted with feel-good products (e.g. with ice cream).

OVERVIEW OF CHAPTERS

The following chapter will provide a review from the behavioral literatures on affective states and emotion regulation. Also in Chapter 2, the conceptual framework for this research is discussed. Chapter 3 comprises the development and statement of

11

hypotheses in this research, a description of the studies performed to test predictions and expected results. Chapter 4 follows with the outcome of the studies conducted. Finally, Chapter 5 provides a discussion of results, contributions to be extracted from this research, as well as concluding remarks.

CHAPTER 2

Literature Review

INTRODUCTION

The consumer research literature is replete with work on the role that affect plays in judgment and choice as well as the exchange that occurs between cognition and affect in information processing (Pham 1998; Schwarz and Clore 1983, 1996; Khan and Isen 1993; Bagozzi, Gopinath and Nyer 1999; Luce, Bettman and Payne 2001; Walther and Grigoriadis 2004). Furthermore, scholars have investigated how affective responses influence attitudes (Cohen and Arenia 1991; Williams and Aaker 2002) and stimulate purchase behavior (Bagozzi and Moore 1994; Burke and Edell 1989; Derbaix 1995; Moore and Harris 1996). Other consumer researchers have studied how certain elements in the retail environment influence mood (Bitner 1992; Dawson, Bloch and Ridgway 1990; Faber and Christenson 1996; Gardner 1985; Kelley and Hoffman 1997; Knowles, Grove and Picket 1993; Manrai 1993; Sherman, Mathur and Smith 1997). More recently, a growing number of scholars have begun to examine discrete emotions, such as sadness and pride, and the attitudinal and motivational implications of these various, specific affective states (Louro, Pieters and Zeelenberg 2005; Menon and Dube 2000; Raghunathan and Pham 1999; Vanhamme 2000). Yet and still, limited research has examined how consumers' purchase behavior might be guided by, or used as a mechanism, to manage affective states.

This research explores the role that discrete emotions play in the consumption process by examining how consumers might use consumption as a mechanism for regulating or managing their emotions. First, a general overview of affective states in consumer behavior is provided. Following this, a discussion of emotion regulation is presented along with a review of work in the consumer research literature that has explored this phenomenon. Finally, a theoretical framework is proffered to explain the

emotion regulation phenomenon using Fredrickson's broaden-and-build theory of

positive emotions (1998, 2000, 2001), resource-based approaches to self-regulation and

mood (Aspinwall 1998; Baumeister *et al.*1998) and emotion regulation strategy (Gross

and John 2003). The distinction between affective states and their growing importance in

the consumer research literature is discussed next.

AFFECTIVE STATES IN CONSUMER BEHAVIOR

The words affect, mood and emotions have been used interchangeably in

behavioral research (Bower and Forgas 2000). However, as work in the social sciences

has begun to examine subjective feelings in more detail, the terms have become more

differentiated (Parkinson, Totterdell, Briner ad Reynolds 1996; Fredrickson 2001;

Raghunathan and Corfman 2004). Theoretical differences do exist between the terms.

These distinctions are delineated next.

Affect is the most general of the three terms and is a superordinate category for

affective states[1]. Both mood and emotions are inherent in affect. Affect is often

conceptualized along two dimensions, positive versus negative or pleasantness versus

arousal (Fredrickson 2001). Consumer researchers have studied affect in advertising

(Chen, Harris and Moore 1995), the supremacy of affect over cognition (Pham, Cohen,

Pracejus and Hughes 2002), and affect in decision-making (Kahn and Isen 1993).

Mood is more differentiated than affect and less intense than emotions. Moods

are often longer lasting and more diffuse than emotions (Parkinson, Totterdell, Briner and

Reynolds 1996). Individuals may not be consciously aware of their mood (Bower and

Forgas 2000). Moods can also be induced subtly by changes in the weather, waking or

---

[1] Throughout this research, the term affect may be used generically to refer to moods or emotions.

sleeping. Although moods are less intense than emotions, a series and consistent pattern of experiencing the same emotion can develop into a mood. For example, multiple experiences of sadness may develop into a depressive mood state. Faber and Christenson (1996) studied mood with regard to compulsive shoppers. Gardener (1985) observed how factors in the retail environment as well as promotions could affect the mood of consumers. These mood states may be affected by service encounters, point-of-purchase stimuli, the content of marketing commutations, and the context of communications. Furthermore, Gardner proposed that moods could influence behavior, bias evaluations and enhance recall in mood congruent directions.

Emotions, unlike moods are more intense and ephemeral. Emotions are response tendencies to a stimulus. They have an antecedent, or cause. Emotions involve a higher degree of cognitive awareness than moods (Smith and Ellsworth 1985; Lazarus 1984, 1991) and may manifest themselves in facial expressions (Izard 1977). Further, unlike affect and mood, emotions are grouped into discrete categories or taxonomies such as anger, fear, pride and joy (Izard 1977; Plutchik 1980).

Specifically, the study of individual or discrete emotions has special implications for consumer research because various emotions may influence attitudes and motivation (Scherer 1984; Roseman *et al.* 1990; Lerner and Keltner 2000). For example, emotions have been found to have adaptive and functional significance in human survival (Izard 1977; Plutchik 1980). Fridja (1986) proposed that different emotions produce action tendencies within the individual, or states of readiness. Anger promotes the action tendency to attack, while fear the action tendency to escape. Hence, emotions incite action (Gross 2005). Further, Lazarus (1984, 1991) and Smith and Ellsworth (1985) suggested that certain emotions result in different appraisals of the environment. An emotion like sadness creates an appraisal or awareness of loss, while an emotion like pride, an appraisal of achievement.

Holbrook and Hirschman (1982) cautioned against consumer researchers only choosing to pursue the study of global affect when studying affective states; thus, they encouraged the study of the full gamut of emotions. This has particular significance since specific emotions may impact attitudes and motivation differently. For example, Raghunathan and Pham (1999) explored the qualitative differences between different affective states (anxiety and sadness) of the same valence and found that different affective states of the same valence have different effects on motivation and decision-making (Raghunathan and Corfman 2003).

Presently, a growing number of scholars have begun to examine the role that discrete emotions play in the consumption process (Garg, Wansink and Inman 2007; Richins 1997; Louro, Pieters, Zeelenberg 2005; Raghunathan and Pham 1999; Garg, Inman and Mittal 1995). Examining specific emotions has garnered interest among consumer researchers because different affective states such as amusement, sadness and anger result in distinct meaning and appraisals and might have unique motivational implications on choice and decision-making. Pursuing this course of study by gaining further understanding about the role that emotions have in the consumption process also contributes to acquiring further insight into ERC.

EMOTION REGULATION

Emotion regulation refers to a process by which individuals attempt to influence "the emotions they have, when they have them and how these emotions are experienced

17

and expressed" (Gross *et al.* p. 3). This process can be automatic or unconscious, such as hiding the anger one feels when rejected by a peer, or controlled and conscious, such as restraining oneself from an emotional outburst after being cutoff in traffic. However, most emotion regulation might be conceptualized on a continuum from conscious, effortful, and controlled regulation to unconscious, effortless and automatic regulation (Gross *et al.* 2006).

An individual may engage in emotion regulation to dampen, intensify, or simply maintain an existing emotion (Gross 2005). Emotion regulation differs from coping, in that coping's principal focus is on decreasing negative affect, caused by life events (e.g. coping with bereavement) for larger periods of time (Gross *et al.* 2006). Emotion regulation is focused on primarily managing an individual's subjective state, rather than objective circumstances (Larsen 2000).

Convention suggests that individuals would rather feel good than bad (Clark and Isen 1982; Isen 1984). Lazarus (1991) suggested that when experiencing negative emotions, people try to improve their emotional state. Negative emotions are the emotions most commonly regulated, with individuals making proactive attempts to "down-regulate," or minimize negative experiential states (Andrade 2005; Catanzaro and Mearns 1990; Morris and Reilly 1987; Gross *et al.* 2006; Fredrickson and Branigan 2001; Baumeister 2002; Faber and Christenson 1996; Weaver and Laird 1995; Zillman 1988).

For example, Cialdini, Darby and Vincent (1973) developed the negative relief model, which proposes that one can relieve negative affective states by subjecting oneself to a positive reinforcing state. Underwood, Moore and Rosenhan (1973) suggested that individuals can alleviate negative moods by managing the emotion created by the

18

stressor, redefining the significance of the stressful event, or taking action to eliminate the stressful factor. Franko, Powers, Zuroff and Moskowitz (1985) proposed a generalized expectancy theory of affect regulation. By interviewing children and asking them to describe a situation in which they felt angry or sad, they found that the children were able to produce solutions to their dilemmas, indicating that affect regulation may be a learned problem-solving behavior that manifests itself early in human development.

Additionally, people experiencing negative emotions may engage in various self-indulgent acts as therapy to down-regulate negative emotions (Morris and Reilly 1987; Mick and Demoss 1990; Babin, Darden and Griffith 1995; Tice Bratslavsky and Baumeister 2001; Thayer 1996). Baumeister (2002) suggested that sad individuals might show an increase in gratifying consumption, such as eating more snack foods, purchasing music CDs or flashy clothes, as well as impulsive spending. Manucia, Baumann and Cialdini (1984) discovered increased helping and altruism among saddened subjects, another possible response behavior instrumental in mitigating negative affective states. Additionally, Meadowcraft and Zillmann (1987) observed that women in premenstrual and menstrual phases, a period in which negative emotions prevail, preferred comedy programs to action dramas.

Individuals might also self-regulate positive emotions in an effort to maintain positive feelings (Isen and Simmonds 1978; Pearlin and Schooler 1978). Isen (1984, 1985, and 2000) suggested that individuals are generally motivated to maintain, even prolong, pleasant affective states; however, affect control processes are likely to be more apparent in sad individuals than happy individuals because of the urgent need to dispel negative feelings. As discussed previously, individuals may engage in a number of

19

behaviors, one of which may be consumption, to alleviate negative emotion. The next section provides a review of the literature that addresses consumption activities that might be construed as behavior to manage, or regulate, emotions.

EMOTION REGULATION IN CONSUMER RESEARCH

Affective states exert considerable influence on behavior, judgment and recall (Isen 1984). The consumer research literature has studied to some degree how individuals might engage in behavior to manage negative affective states. For example, purchasing a product with some hedonic benefit might help a consumer in overcoming a negative affective state. Consumption of these products can help divert attention away from negative feelings and allow refocusing (Kacen 1994). Rook and Gardener (1989) and Gardner and Scott (1990) found that individuals often use the purchase of material goods to perpetuate a desired mood or to alleviate a negative one.

Faber and Christensen (1996) examined mood and compulsive shopping. Their research followed Faber and O'Guinn (1989), which employed a phenomenological approach to the study of compulsive shopping. Faber and Christensen (1996) compared mood states of both compulsive shoppers and noncompulsive shoppers during a shopping experience. Both groups were subjected to a survey and interview by psychiatric professionals. Findings indicated that compulsive shoppers reported experiencing more positive moods during shopping than noncompulsive shoppers. Conversely, noncompulsive shoppers reported experiencing more positive moods before shopping than during shopping. These results suggest that the compulsive shoppers may have been using shopping as a form of self-medication.

20

Elliot (1994) found further evidence for the use of shopping as a mechanism for managing affect among compulsive shoppers. Compulsive buying was highly correlated with a mood repair scale developed by Elliot to determine the degree to which shopping alleviated depressive mood states. Both Faber and Christensen (1996) and Elliot's (1994) research provides some insight into how a segment of individuals (compulsive shoppers) might use shopping and purchasing as a way to manage mood, or regulate emotions.

Mick and DeMoss (1990) examined more typical consumer behavior by studying self-gifting. A self-gift is a product or service an individual purchases for themselves. Self-gifting is a consumption activity that consumers may pursue in order to perpetuate a desired affective state, or to alleviate a negative one. These gifts provide some hedonic benefit to the consumer and may be construed as rewarding or therapeutic.

Applying a phenomenological approach to the study of self-gifting, Mick and DeMoss (1990) found self-gifts to be a form of self-communication, to be context bound and to be a form of therapy or a reward. Self-gifts were purchased by informants to communicate to oneself, facilitate an exchange, as well as to confer something special. As a form of communication, self-gifts were protective to self-esteem and identity. In this context, the consumer acts as both sender and receiver of symbolic messages to the self. For example, in Mick and Demoss' study, a woman who had just quit her job treated herself to a new hairstyle as a confidence builder. Self-gifts may also be purchased as an exchange for hard work performed. Another individual in the study treated herself to a day at the spa for completing a marathon. Finally, self-gifts may be purchased because they are simply special and unique. Another informant in the study embarked on a trip to the Orient for its specialness and uniqueness. The work by Mick

21

and DeMoss (1990) suggests that typical consumers may engage in affect or emotion regulation by purchasing products that are characteristically hedonic. Other consumer researchers have also observed that hedonic products can be both therapeutic and useful in mood management (Babin *et al.* 1994).

More recent studies of affect regulation have examined food consumption as a mechanism for regulating emotions. Andrade (2005) found that women that were induced to feel positive and negative affect (versus neutral) expressed stronger behavioral intentions to try chocolate. Garg, Wansink and Inman (2007) studied how affect (happiness and sadness) influences food consumption. They found evidence for the prevalence of food consumption as a mood management tactic in both women and men. In three experimental studies, consumption of hedonic foods (e.g. buttered popcorn and M&Ms) was used to manage the emotion of subjects that were induced to feel happy or sad. Consumption, however, was moderated by the presence of nutritional information in both the sad and neutral conditions.

An individual's inherent ability to engage in emotion regulation may also affect his or her purchase behavior. Babin and Darden (1995) studied self-regulation in the retail environment and attributes in consumers that might cause them to respond to emotional arousal differently. Using Kuhl's Action Control Theory as a conceptual framework, they examined both state-oriented consumers and action oriented-consumers. According to Kuhl's Action Control Theory (1986), state-oriented individuals are less likely to exercise regulatory control over arousal and contextual influences, whereas action-oriented individuals are more likely to exercise control over arousal and contextual influences. In a cross-sectional study, Babin and Darden (1995) found that state-oriented consumers spent more money than action-oriented consumers when in a highly arousing environment. Hence, Babin and Darden's research suggests that individual differences in emotional regulatory behavior can influence purchase behavior. More recent research in psychology (Koole and Jostmann 2004) has found that action-oriented individuals manage or "down-regulate" negative affect through intuitive cognitive processes better than state-oriented individuals.

As mentioned previously, pursuing the study of specific emotions, beyond global affect, has special significance for consumer research. Richins (1997) developed the Consumption Emotions Scale (CES) because of the dearth of instruments available in consumer behavior to measure emotions. The CES captures 13 emotions purported to be experienced by consumers in the consumption process: anger, fear, sadness, shame, guilt, worry, envy, loneliness, contentment, romantic love, optimism and peacefulness.

Richins compared the CES to commonly used instruments that measure emotions in the consumer research literature and found that these measures [Differential Emotions Scale (Izard 1977), Emotion Profile Index (Plutchik 1980), Pleasure Arousal Dominance Scale (Mehrabian and Russell 1974), Edell and Burke's (1987) and Batra and Holbrook's (1990) scales that assess affective states elicited by advertising] were all inadequate when researchers desired to measure a broad assessment of emotions in the consumption experience. Richins work lends credence to the viewpoint that consumers experience different and discrete emotions in the consumption process and encourages consumer researchers to gain more insight into the dynamics of consumption and emotions. Several researchers have assumed this course of study.

Mano (1999) examined boredom and distress and the affect that these affective states have in the shopping environment. Results suggested that when bored subjects were offered the prospect of shopping in a favorable environment (with good service quality), they expressed higher purchase intentions; however when offered the prospect of shopping in an uncomfortable environment (bad service quality), they expressed lower purchase intentions. Further, overall distressed subjects exhibited higher purchase intentions than their bored counterparts. Thus, Mano demonstrated the importance of understanding pre-existing emotions and how these emotions may indeed be factors that influence purchase behavior in the shopping environment.

Bagozzi *et al.* (2000) proposed that positive consumption-related emotions stimulate subsequent positive behaviors such as repurchase. However, more recent research has provided evidence that different emotions of the same valence may have different impacts on behavior and decision-making (Raghunathan and Pham 2002; Raghunathan, and 2004; Garg, Inman and Mittal 2005). Specifically, Louro *et al.* (2005) studied the positive emotion, pride. They found that the effect of pride on consumers' repurchase intentions is contingent on self-regulatory goals. Consumers with high prevention pride were less likely to repurchase than those with high promotion pride.

As stated earlier, individuals are driven by strong motivations to mitigate unpleasant feelings. But are these driving forces conscious or controlled? There is evidence to suggest that the strategies that individuals use to manage or alter affective states are often controlled and conscious (Clark and Isen 1982; Posner and Snyder 1975). Cohen and Andrade (2004) found that individuals are somewhat aware, or at least were able to provide a naïve theory about pursuing proactive attempts to change their affective state. When subjects were asked why they selected certain mood-inducing songs that where either imbued with sad or happy emotions, subjects were able to theorize that they were doing it to regulate a certain feeling state.

The consumer research literature offers evidence for the ERC phenomenon. People may shop and purchase special gifts for themselves to alleviate negative affective states. Also, specific emotions are experienced in the consumption process and may have different effects on decision-making and behavior. Further, individual differences in emotional regulatory behavior can influence purchase behavior. The next section offers a guiding conceptual framework for explaining the ERC phenomenon.

CONCEPTUAL FRAMEWORK

In this section, theoretical insight is proffered to illuminate why, under what circumstances, and when consuming to regulate emotions might occur using Fredrickson's broaden-and-build theory of positive emotions (1998, 2000, 2001) and resource-based approaches to mood and self-regulation (Aspinwall 1997, 1998; Muraven, Tice and Baumeister 1998; Baumeister 2002). In addition, one emotion regulation strategy, cognitive reappraisal, from the work of Gross and John (2003) is introduced to the consumer research literature to further explain the emotion regulation consumption phenomenon.

Broaden-and-Build Theory of Positive Emotions

The broaden-and-build theory of positive emotions (Fredrickson 1998, 2000, 2001) helps to elucidate why consumers might engage in consumption activity to regulate emotions, particularly negative emotion. The theory proposes that positive emotions such as joy, interest, and love have the ability to *broaden* thought-action repertoire. This

25

broadening occurs by augmenting an individual's scope of attention, cognition and action. Moreover, the theory postulates that positive emotions can also *build* psychological, social, intellectual and physical resources. Finally, the broaden-and-build theory asserts that positive emotions can "undo" the effects of negative emotions.

The broadening of thought-action repertoire proposition of the broaden-and-build theory has found some support in the work of Derryberry and Tucker's (1994). In studying manic people (individuals experiencing elated mood states), they discovered that in a global-local visual processing task these individuals tended to use "overinclusive categories" by creatively grouping seemingly unrelated items together (Kimchi 1992). Other researchers have found that positive affect enlarges cognitive context and makes individuals more variety seeking (Carnevale and Isen, 1986; Isen, Daubman and Nowicki 1987; Isen and Khan 1993).

In contrast, while positive emotions broaden thought-action repertoire, negative emotions narrow thought-action repertoire. Previous emotion theorists have studied the adaptive and functional quality of emotions (Izard 1977; Plutchik 1980; Fridja 1986) finding that negative emotions engender the narrowing of cognitive abilities and are essential to survival. For example, anger narrows thought-action abilities and enlists action tendencies to attack; similarly, fear activates the propensity to escape from harm or danger.

Positive emotions also build physical, intellectual, psychological and social resources. For example, positive emotions are instrumental in creating the urge to play, which helps in building physical resources and motor skills (Pelligrini 1987). These physical resources can be drawn on later in emergencies. Positive emotions also build

26

social resources though shared experiences and social play. Research has found that those experiencing positive emotions are prone to helping others (Isen and Simmonds 1978; Isen and Geva 1987).

In addition, positive emotions build psychological resources by developing resilience and optimism. They function as restorers, helping to replenish resources that have been depleted by stress. Fredrickson and Joiner (2003) have linked positive emotions to a style of coping characterized by taking a broader perspective on problems and seeing beyond immediate stressors. Supporting this viewpoint, Fredrickson Tugade, Waugh and Larkin (2003) found that positive emotions in the aftermath of crisis buffered resilient people against depression and fueled thriving.

Finally, according to the broaden-and-build theory, positive emotions build intellectual resources. Carnevale and Isen (1986) found that individuals given bags of candy could better comprehend a complex, integrative bargaining task.

Specifically related to emotion regulation, the broaden-and-build theory proposes that positive emotions have the ability to "undo" the effect of negative emotions. Physiological support was found for this phenomenon (Frederickson and Levenson 1998; Fredrickson, Mancuso, Branigan and Tugade 2000). In a study conducted by Fredrickson *et al.* (2000), participants were exposed to an anxiety-inducing task. Following the task, they were shown one of four films that elicited the following emotions: contentment, amusement, sadness and neutrality. Those subjects in the positive emotion induction conditions (amusement and contentment) experienced a faster return to baseline cardiovascular reactivity than those participants shown films that elicited the negative emotion (sadness), and those in the control (neutral condition). These findings lend

27

support to the undoing hypothesis. Ergo, positive emotions may enable individuals to "down-regulate" or "undo" the effects of negative emotions.

Evidence from the consumer research literature has demonstrated that individuals may engage in purchase or consumption behavior to down-regulate or decrease negative emotions felt (Garg, Wansink, Inman 2007; Andrade 2005; Elliot 1994; Mick amd DeMoss 1990; Faber and Christensen 1996; Mano 1999). Products that facilitate or perpetuate feelings of enjoyment are often referred to as hedonic products (Holbrook and Hirshman 1986; Hirshman and Holbrook 1986; Dhar and Wertenbroch 2000; Voss, Spangenberg and Grohmann 2003). Hedonic products often generate positive affective responses from the consumer. Subsequently, individuals experiencing negative emotions may be making attempts to infuse positive emotions into their lives by consuming products from which they derive some hedonic benefit.

In summary, the broaden-and-build theory of positive emotions proposes that positive emotions have the ability to *broaden* thought-action repertoire as well as *build* psychological, social, intellectual and physical resources. Importantly, the undoing hypothesis of the theory provides theoretical support as to why individuals experiencing negative emotions may be inclined to engage in consumption to "down-regulate" negative emotions through consumption. The following section offers theoretical justification as to the circumstances and conditions in which emotion regulation might occur.

Self-Regulation and Mood-as-a-Resource Hypothesis

Consumption behavior can also be affected by the degree to which an individual can engage in self-regulation. Controlling one's own behavior can exhaust an

28

individual's self-regulatory resources. These resources, which operate like energy or strength, help direct responses (Baumeister *et al.* 1998; Vohs, Baumeister and Ciarocco 2005; Vohs and Heatherton 2000) and are put into use when an individual attempts to modify, alter or change his/her behavior. Self-regulatory resources can be reduced with use, and when various demands deplete these resources, individuals may fail at self-control (Muraven and Baumeister 2000). For example, emotional duress can contribute to a breakdown in self-control. (Baumeister et al. 1998; Tice et al. 1998; Muraven and Baumeister 2000).

Baumeister *et al.* (1998) demonstrated how inner resources could be depleted in several studies using temptation and impulse control. In one condition, participants that had skipped a meal were seated in front of chocolates and cookies and told to refrain from partaking of any of the chocolates and cookies, but were told to help themselves to a bowl of radishes. The participants in this condition gave up much faster on a subsequent geometric figure-tracing exercise, compared to participants in either of two control groups (one of which was permitted to eat the cookies and chocolates, and the other of which was never exposed to food of any kind). Resisting temptation depleted the self's resources, leaving it nearly unable to persist in an ensuing self-control task.

Baumeister *et al.* (1998) refer to the depletion of resources as ego depletion. Ego depletion describes the condition whereby, the self's resources are expended and the self is temporarily operating at less than full capacity. Coping with negative affect may lead to poor self-regulation (Muraven and Baumeister 2000). When people are upset, the goal of feeling better often takes precedence over self-control. People may eat unhealthy foods, procrastinate or seek immediate gratification (Muraven and Baumeister 2000;

29

Baumeister 2002; Tice, Bratslavsky and Baumeister 2001). Vohs and Faber (2002) found that depleting consumers of attentional, emotional or mental self-control could result in impulse buying.

Impulse buying is a sudden and compelling purchasing behavior that offers immediate hedonic benefit (Puri 1996). Rook (1987) defined impulse buying as "an unplanned purchase" that is characterized by quick decision-making and subjective bias in favor of immediate possession. Beatty and Ferrell (1998) indicated that impulse buying includes an overwhelming urge to buy. Kacen and Lee (2002) explained impulse buying as a "sudden, hedonically complex purchasing behavior" (p.164). Hoch and Loewenstetin (1991) characterized impulse buying as a contest between desire and willpower.

In sum, the impulse purchase decision process precludes thoughtful, deliberate consideration of information and results in the immediate acquisition of a product or service. It often involves deviation from a decision that the decision maker intended to make beforehand or one in which they typically make (Dholakia, Gapinath and Bagozzzi 2000).

Consumer mood and emotional state may influence impulse buying behavior (Beatty and Ferrell 1998; Donovan , Rossiter, Marcoolyn and Nesdale 1994; Rook 1987.). Seeman and Schwarz (1974) and Schwarz and Pollack (1977) demonstrated that children in whom a positive affective state had been induced were better able to delay gratification better than children in whom a negative affective state had been induced. Fry (1975) found that children in a positive affective state were better able to resist temptation to play with a forbidden toy than were children in a negative affective state.

30

Further, in a study that investigated the phenomenology of impulse buying, respondents indicated that the impulse buying made them feel good, happy, satisfied, light, wonderful or high (Rook 1987). Those that had been feeling down added that it made them feel better. In another study, Rook and Gardner (1993) found that happy and sad subjects were more likely to buy on impulse than subjects in more neutral affective states. Additionally, Cohen and Andrade (2004) proposed that remaining in a negative emotional state is likely to activate mood-repair responses such as impulsive purchasing.

Positive emotions may affect self-regulation by influencing a person's immediate psychological resources as well as determine how the self-control dilemma is resolved (Aspinwall 1998; Trope and Neter 1994). Individuals that possess a reserve of positive emotions may be less likely to engage in impulsive buying. Aspinwall's (1997, 1998) resource-based approach to self-regulation predicts that if a level of self-regard, positive emotions or subjective well-being is enjoyed above some threshold, a *hedonic surplus* exists. However, if self-worth and subjective well-being have been reduced so that they fall below a certain threshold, a *hedonic deficit* may be experienced, and these individuals may be more likely to engage in mood repair.

Positive emotions may also influence a person's appraisals of their resources to withstand negative events and information (Isen 1970; Schwarz and Bohner 1996). In the information processing literature, positive emotions have been found to act as a buffer, or resource, against negative information (Raghunathan and Trope 2002). Trope and Pomerantz (1998) proposed that the presence of positive mood changes the weight of immediate costs relative to long-term gains. In several studies, they found that positive

31

experiences increased the likelihood of individuals accepting feedback, even when it had the potential of spoiling an existing positive mood.

Applying self-regulation and the mood-as-a-resource framework in a consumption context, individuals with a reserve of positive emotions may be less likely to engage in certain forms of consumption that represent attempts to down-regulate negative emotion. However, when a consumer's resources have been depleted, he/she may fail to exercise self-control. These individuals may be more likely to engage in hedonic consumption to help restore depleted resources. A breakdown in self-control or regulation may result in consumption behavior that is impulsive and possibly excessive (Pechmann *et al.* 2005). Yet, there may be inherent differences or characteristics in individuals that render them less likely to engage in consumption as a way of restoring depleted resources or even down-regulating negative emotion. This may be linked to cognitive processes they employ to regulate emotion, which will be discussed next.

Emotions Regulation Strategy

Individual differences in the way that consumers regulate their emotions may affect their consumption behavior. Research from the psychology literature suggests that individuals can cognitively exercise control over their emotions by using strategies to influence which emotions they experience and when they have them (Lazarus and Alfert 1964). One common emotion regulation strategy is *cognitive reappraisal* (Gross and John 1998), which can manifest itself as a trait, or individual difference.

Lazarus and Folkman (1984) proposed that individuals can cope with emotion through cognitive maneuvers, which alter the meaning of an event (Lazarus 1966, 1975). These maneuvers, known as cognitive reappraisal, are a form of cognitive change that

32

involves construing a potentially emotion-eliciting situation in a way that changes its emotional impact (Lazarus and Alfert 1964). Reappraisal is an antecedent–focused strategy, in that it occurs early and intervenes before the emotion response tendencies have been fully activated. Cognitive reappraisal can alter the entire emotion trajectory. When used to down-regulate emotion, it reduces the behavioral consequences of negative emotion. One common application of cognitive change in the social domain is downward social comparison, which involves comparing one's situation with that of a less fortunate person, altering one's construal and decreasing negative emotions (Taylor and Lobel 1989).

Research has found that individuals engaging in cognitive reappraisal experience and express more positive emotions. High cognitive reappraisers are able to down-regulate the experience of negative emotion more effectively (Gross and John 2003). Subsequently, individuals that use reappraisal often show enhanced functioning in interpersonal situations.

ERC may be contingent on an individual's proclivity to employ an emotion regulation strategy to alter a specific emotion. Specifically, individuals with a propensity to engage in cognitive reappraisal when experiencing a negative emotion may be able to reduce the behavioral consequences of negative emotion. Consequently, they may be less compelled to engage in certain forms of consumption to down-regulate a negative emotion. Additionally, those engaging in cognitive reappraisal frequently may enjoy a certain level of subjective well-being—possessing a hedonic surplus—which may place them in a situation where they are less likely to engage in impulsive buying behavior.

SUMMARY

Emotions are discrete entities with distinct meaning and motivational implications; thus, studying emotion is important because different emotions may result in different types of consumption behavior. Studying discrete emotions also enhances understanding of the emotion regulation phenomenon, particularly because individuals may engage in different activities to manage specific emotions.

Evidence suggests that individuals would typically rather feel good than bad and may use consumption to improve their emotional state. The broaden-and-build theory, resource-based approaches to self-regulation and mood, as well as individual differences in emotion regulation strategy all have a great deal of potential to contribute to the consumer research literature in providing theoretical explanation for the ERC phenomenon. The broaden-and-build theory explains how positive emotions such as joy, interest, and contentment can mitigate negative emotions. Individuals may engage in hedonic consumption to invoke positive emotion; thereby, "undoing" or down-regulating the effects of negative emotions.

The self-regulation model of ego depletion and the mood-as-a-resource hypothesis helps to provide insight regarding under what circumstances and contexts emotion regulation consumption might occur. Individuals possessing a hedonic surplus may exhibit higher levels of self-control, and may be less compelled to engage in emotion regulation consumption; however, those experiencing a hedonic deficit might experience self-regulatory failure and be more inclined to consume products of a hedonic nature to achieve short-term gratification.

In addition, examining individual differences in emotion regulation might help to explain which individuals might be more likely to engage in ERC. Individuals with a propensity for engaging in cognitive reappraisal may be less likely to consume products when presented with a negative situation.

In this research, three experiments addressed research questions regarding emotion regulation through consumption. Because individuals are typically driven to mitigate unpleasant feelings, this research examined whether individuals that were experiencing negative emotion were more likely to engage in hedonic consumption than those experiencing positive emotion. Furthermore, these studies examined whether emotion regulation strategy interacted with the effect of emotions to influence behavioral intentions and other related variables toward a hedonic product.

Theory also suggests that when an individual exerts a great deal of effort on a task or undergoes emotional duress, the motivation may be greater to purchase products to down-regulate negative emotions. At times, individuals may engage in consumption of an impulsive nature to achieve gratification in the short-term. Positive emotions may have an adaptive quality in helping to prevent individuals from engaging in impulsive purchase behavior (Tice *et al.* 2006). This research examined whether individuals experiencing negative emotions that were subjected to an ego depletion task were more likely to engage in impulsive hedonic consumption than those experiencing positive emotion that were subjected to the same task.

In the following chapter, hypotheses in this research are stated and theoretically substantiated, the methodology used to test predictions is discussed and expected results are explicated.

35

CHAPTER 3

Methodology

INTRODUCTION

The conceptualization, hypothesis development, methodology and expected results of three experimental studies will be delineated in this chapter. These studies provide empirical evidence in helping to examine emotion regulation consumption (ERC), or the consumption or purchase of a good or service for the purposes of alleviating, repairing, or managing an affective state. This research helps to corroborate that ERC is a common occurrence in the lives of individuals. Specifically, the first study tested whether individuals that are experiencing a negative emotion (sadness) are more likely to engage in the purchase of hedonic goods than those experiencing a positive emotion (amusement). Additionally, the moderating role of emotion regulation strategy was ascertained. This research question was examined using a 3 (emotions: amusement/neutrality/sadness) X 2 (cognitive reappraisal: low/high) between-subjects experimental design.

The second study in this research examined the effect of emotions, self-regulation, and emotion regulation strategy on impulse control. The study tested whether emotions and ego depletion had an effect on impulsive hedonic purchase behavior. A 2 (ego depletion task: present/absent) X 3 (emotion: contentment/ neutrality/fear and anxiety) X 2 (cognitive reappraisal: low/high) between-subjects design was used to test predictions. Finally, the third study was similar to Study 2 and employed a 2 (ego depletion task: present /absent) X 3 (amusement/neutrality/sadness) X 2(cognitive reappraisal: low/high); however, actual behavior was assessed by giving subjects the option of engaging in a purchase decision task.

BACKGROUND AND HYPOTHESES

Acts of emotion regulation are essential to facilitating social exchanges and contributing to the functioning of a civilized society (Gross and Thompson 2005). Emotion regulation refers to a process by which individuals make concerted efforts to influence the emotions they have, when they have them and how these emotions are experienced and expressed (Gross, Richards and John 2006).

Affect regulation theories have proposed ways in which people regulate or manage their emotions. Cialdini, Darby and Vincent's (1973) negative relief model postulates that one can relieve negative affective states by subjecting oneself to a positive reinforcing state. Underwood, Moore and Rosenhan (1973) suggested that individuals alleviate negative moods by managing the emotion created by the stressor, redefining stressful events, or eliminating stressful factors. Franko *et al.* (1985) proposed a generalized expectancy theory of affect regulation, suggesting among other things that affect regulation is a learned problem-solving behavior, which manifests itself early in human development.

The outcome of emotion regulation may vary. Individuals may regulate positive emotions in an effort to maintain positive feelings, or make proactive attempts to "down-regulate" or dispel negative emotions (Isen and Simmonds 1978; Pearlin and Schooler 1978; Isen 1984, 1985, and 2000). Prior research suggests that negative emotions are the most commonly regulated emotions (Lazarus 1991; Clark and Isen 1982; Isen 1984; Andrade 2005; Catanzaro and Mearns 1990; Morris and Reilly 1987; Gross, Richards, John 2006; Fredrickson and Branigan 2001; Baumeister 2002; Faber and Christenson 1996; Weaver and Laird 1995; Zillman 1988). Because individuals are driven by strong motivations to mitigate unpleasant feelings, their behavior to allay these unpleasant feelings may be guided by the discrepancy between what they feel in the present and what they may feel in the future as a result of a certain behavioral activity (Andrade 2005; Gross 1998). Consequently, in some instances, consumers may purchase products of a hedonic nature to make themselves feel better. This mechanism for managing emotions is referred to as emotion regulation consumption (ERC) in this research. Emotion regulation consumption refers specifically to the consumption or purchase of a good or service for the purpose of alleviating, repairing, or managing an affective state.

The consumer research literature has studied to some degree how individuals might engage in regulatory behavior to manage negative affective states (Garg, Wansink, Inman 2007; Andrade 2005; Elliot 1994; Mick and DeMoss 1990; Faber and Christenson 1996; Mano 1999). For example, Faber and Christensen (1996) compared mood states of both compulsive shoppers and noncompulsive shoppers during a shopping experience and found that compulsive shoppers may have been using shopping as a way to manage or alleviate negative emotions. Elliot (1994) also found evidence for the use of shopping as an emotion regulation mechanism among compulsive shoppers. Specifically, compulsive shopping was found to be highly correlated with a mood repair scale developed by Elliot to determine the degree to which shopping alleviated depressive mood states.

While compulsive buying is an extreme, abnormal consumption behavior, other consumer researchers have demonstrated that consumption of products to improve mood may exist in more typical and conventional contexts. Mick and DeMoss (1990) examined self-gifting. Self-gifts can be rewards and incentives for personal

39

achievements, consolation prizes for disappointment, or holiday gifts (Tournier 1966; Mick and Demoss 1990). Mick and DeMoss found that self-gifting provided some hedonic benefit to the consumer, and in many cases these gifts were construed as rewarding or therapeutic.

More recent studies of affect regulation have examined food consumption as a mechanism for regulating emotions. Andrade (2005) found that women that were induced to feel positive and negative affect (versus neutral) expressed stronger behavioral intentions to eat chocolate. Further, Garg, Wansink and Inman (2007) studied how specific emotions, happiness and sadness, influenced food consumption. They found evidence for the pervasiveness of food consumption as a mood management tactic for both genders.

Broaden-and-Build Theory of Positive Emotions

Previously, affect regulation theories have proffered that individuals are motivated to regulate emotions, particularly negative ones (Cialdini, Darby and Vincent 1973; Underwood, Moore and Rosenhan 1973; Franko *et al.*1985; Morris and Reilly 1987). Fredrickson's broaden-and-build theory of positive emotions extends many of these conceptual arguments by providing physiological support for the emotion regulation phenomenon and illuminating the adaptive quality of positive emotions.

The broaden-and-build theory proposes that positive emotions such as joy, interest, and love have the ability to *broaden* thought-action repertoire. This broadening occurs by augmenting an individual's scope of attention, cognition and action. Additionally, the theory postulates that positive emotions can *build* psychological, social, intellectual and physical resources.

40

Specifically related to emotion regulation, the broaden-and-build theory proposes that positive emotions have the ability to "undo" the effect of negative emotions (Frederickon and Levenson 1998; Fredrickson, Mancuso, Branigan and Tugade 2000). In a study conducted by Fredrickson *et al.* (2000), participants were exposed to an anxiety-inducing task. Following the task, they were shown one of four films that elicited the following emotions: contentment, amusement, sadness and a neutral or control condition. Those subjects in the positive emotion induction conditions (amusement and contentment) experienced a faster return to baseline cardiovascular reactivity than those participants shown films that elicited the negative emotion (sadness) and those in the control (neutral) condition. These findings lend support to the undoing hypothesis. Subsequently, positive emotions may enable individuals to "down-regulate" or "undo" the effects of negative emotions.

The broaden-and-build theory of positive emotions (Fredrickson 1998, 2000, 2001) helps to explain why consumers might engage in consumption activity to regulate emotions, particularly negative emotion. These individuals may be making attempts to infuse positive emotions into their lives by consuming products from which they derive some hedonic benefit.

Mood-as-a-Resource Hypothesis

Although individuals experiencing negative emotions may be motivated to use consumption as a short-term solution to alleviating negative affective states, individuals that possess a reserve of positive emotions may be less likely to engage in immediate gratification or purely hedonic pursuits. Aspinwall's (1997, 1998) resource-based approach to self-regulation predicts that if positive emotions or subjective well-being is

41

enjoyed above a certain threshold, a *hedonic surplus* exists and individuals may subsequently be able to pursue goals other than hedonic pursuits. However, if self-worth and subjective well being have been denigrated so that they fall below a certain threshold, a *hedonic deficit* may result, and these individuals may be more likely to engage in mood repair.

Applying the mood-as-a-resource framework in a consumption context, individuals with a reserve of positive emotions may be less likely to engage in certain forms of consumption that bring about immediate gratification. However, those without a reserve of positive emotions, or who may be experiencing negative emotions consistently, may feel an urgent need to engage in affect repair. These individuals may be more likely to engage in hedonic consumption.

In summary, based on the "undoing hypothesis" of the broaden-and-build theory of positive emotions, positive emotions can undo the effects of negative emotions. Subsequently, individuals experiencing negative emotions may engage in various self-gratifying or self-indulgent acts to induce positive emotions in an attempt to down-regulate negative emotions. Specifically, individuals may use consumption as a mechanism for alleviating negative affective states.

Evidence from the consumer research literature suggests that hedonic products can be therapeutic and useful in mood management (Mick and Demoss 1990; Babin Darden and Griffin 1994). Because individuals experiencing negative emotion may have strong motivations to feel better, their evaluations or attitudes towards products with hedonic characteristics may be particularly favorable (Bazerman and Wade-Benzoni 1998; Dhar and Wertenbroch 2000; Loewenstein 1996; Wade-Benzoni 1998).

Further, these individuals may exhibit high purchase intentions and less price sensitivity toward these products (Dhar and Wertenbroch 2000; Mick, DeMoss and Faber 1992). Previous work examining hedonic consumption (choosing a hedonic good over a utilitarian good) found that individuals were willing to pay more in time for a hedonic good than a utilitarian good, and more in money for a utilitarian good than a hedonic good (Okada 2005). However, no affect regulation manipulation was involved in the choice context. Here, it is proposed that the urgency to repair an affective state will make individuals less price sensitive for a hedonic product. Mick, DeMoss and Faber (1996) suggested that in a self-gifting context consumers might be less price sensitive to hedonic products. Dhar and Wertenbroch (2000) suggested that hedonic products rather than utilitarian products can command a price premium.

According to the mood as resource hypothesis, unlike those experiencing positive emotions, individuals experiencing negative emotions are more likely to engage in affect repair. Hence, juxtaposing individuals that are in a negative affective state against those in a positive affective state should result in polarizing effects. Specifically, those in the negative affective state should be more likely to engage in hedonic consumption than those in a positive or neutral affective state. Subsequently, the following is proposed.

H1:   Individuals in a negative emotion condition will express (a) more favorable attitudes, (b) exhibit higher purchase intentions (c) and be willing to pay a higher price for a hedonic good than individuals in a positive emotion condition.

Emotion Regulation Strategy

Individual differences in the way that consumers regulate their emotions may affect their consumption behavior. Research from the psychology literature suggests that individuals can cognitively exercise control over their emotions by using strategies to

43

influence which emotions they experience and when they have them (Lazarus and Alfert 1964). *Cognitive reappraisal* is an emotion regulation strategy that can manifest itself as a trait, or individual difference (Gross and John 1998).

Cognitive reappraisal involves construing a potentially emotion-eliciting situation in a way that changes its emotional impact (Lazarus and Alfert 1964). Reappraisal is an antecedent–focused strategy. It occurs early and intervenes before the emotion response tendencies have been fully triggered. Cognitive reappraisal reduces the behavioral consequences of negative emotion when used to down-regulate emotion. Research has found that individuals engaging in cognitive reappraisal experience and express more (in magnitude) positive emotions (Gross and John 2003).

Emotion regulation consumption may be contingent on an individual's propensity to employ cognitive reappraisal. For example, individuals with a proclivity for engaging in cognitive reappraisal when experiencing a negative emotion may be able to reduce the behavioral consequences of negative emotion. Consequently, they may be less compelled to engage in certain forms of consumption to down-regulate negative emotion. Additionally, those engaging in cognitive reappraisal frequently, may enjoy a certain level of subjective well-being—possessing a hedonic surplus—which may place them in a situation where they may not feel it is necessary to engage in hedonic consumption. The following is proposed:

H2: Emotion regulation strategies will moderate the effect of emotions on attitudes, purchase intentions and price. Low cognitive reappraisers in a negative emotion condition will report (a) more favorable attitudes and (c) express higher purchase intentions (d) and be willing to pay a higher price for a hedonic good than high cognitive reappraisers in a negative emotion condition (see Figure 1).

Self-Regulatory Model

When an individual exerts a great deal of effort on a task or undergoes emotional duress, the motivation may be even greater to purchase products to down-regulate negative emotions. At times, an individual may fail at self-control or self-regulation, even engaging in consumption of an impulsive nature to achieve gratification in the short-term (Vohs and Faber 2002).

Self-regulation involves a single stock of resources that operates like energy or strength (Baumeister et al. 1998; Vohs, Baumeister and Ciarocco 2005; Vohs and Heatherton 2000). When various demands deplete these resources, individuals may fail at self-regulation (Muraven and Baumeister 2000). Baumeister et al. (1998) refer to the depletion of these resources as ego depletion. Ego depletion is a reduced capacity for self-control caused by a prior exercise of self-control (Baumeister et al. 1998). Resisting temptation and regulating emotions can deplete the self's resources. Additionally, coping with negative affect may lead to poor self-regulation (Muraven and Baumeister 2000).

From a consumer research context, ego-depleted individuals may be more likely to engage in impulsive buying behavior because of an inability to exercise self-control (Baumeister 2002). Impulse buying, a process which precludes thoughtful, deliberate consideration of information, results in immediate gratification through the acquisition of a product or service which often deviates from the one the decision maker had intended choosing beforehand, or normally chooses (Dholakia et al. 2005; Hoch and Lowenstein 1991; Kacen and Lee 2002; Puri 1996; Rook 1987). Ego depleted individuals, in particular, may be less likely to resist consumption opportunities of a hedonic nature, thus experiencing strong motivation to restore depleted psychological resources with the

45

positive benefits derived from hedonic products. As a result, they may express more favorable evaluations, feel greater desirability or urges (Dholakia *et al.* 2005) and express higher purchase intentions for these products. In accordance, the following hypotheses are proposed:

H3:   Individuals in an ego depletion condition will exhibit greater levels of buying impulsiveness for a hedonic good than individuals in a no-ego depletion condition.

H4:   Individuals in an ego depletion condition will exhibit (a) more favorable attitudes (b) greater desirability, (c) and higher purchase intentions for a hedonic good than individuals in a no-ego depletion condition.

An individual's affective state may also determine whether they are able to resist an impulsive buying situation (Baumeister 2002). Because positive emotions can help to restore depleted resources (Tice *et al.* 2006), they may affect self-regulation by influencing a person's immediate psychological resources (Aspinwall 1998; Trope and Neter 1994), enabling them to exercise self-control and refrain from impulsive purchases of a hedonic nature. Furthermore, comparing individuals that are experiencing a positive emotion to those experiencing a negative emotion who have both been subjected to an ego depletion task, the following is expected:

H5:   Emotions will moderate the effect of ego depletion in such a way that individuals in an ego depletion condition that are in either a negative or neutral emotion condition will exhibit (a) more favorable attitudes (b) greater desirability, (c) and higher purchase intentions than individuals in a no-ego depletion condition that are in either a negative or neutral emotion condition. However, there will be no differences in attitudes, desirability, and purchase intentions for individuals in a positive emotion condition across an ego and no-ego depletion condition (see Figure 2).

Emotion regulation strategy will also have an effect on hedonic consumption behavior and impulsiveness. Similar to hypothesis 2, low cognitive reappraisers will be

46

more likely to engage in emotion regulation consumption activities. Therefore, emotion regulation strategy is expected to moderate the effect of emotions and ego depletion on attitudes, deisre and purchase intentions in the following way.

H6:   Low cognitive reappraisers in an ego depletion condition that are in either a negative or positive emotion condition will exhibit (a) more favorable attitudes (b) greater desirability, (c) and higher purchase intentions than high cognitive reappraisers in an ego depletion condition that are in either a negative or positive emotion condition. However, there will be no differences in attitudes, desire and purchase intentions between low and high cognitive reappraisers in an ego depletion and neutral emotion condition (see Figure 3).

H7:   Low cognitive reappraisers in an ego depletion and negative emotion condition will exhibit greater levels of buying impulsiveness for a hedonic good than high cognitive reappraisers in a ego depletion and negative emotion condition.

Discrete Emotions

Although the hypotheses enumerated above proposed valence-based effects (positive versus negative) for emotion, discrete affective states will be examined in this research. Pursuing the study of affective states is of significance to consumer research because specific emotions, even of the same valence, may influence attitudes and motivation differently (Scherer 1984; Roseman *et al* 1990; Lerner and Keltner 2000; Raghunathan and Pham 2002; Raghunathan, and 2004; Garg, Inman and Mittal 2005). Further, the psychology literature has demonstrated that emotions have adaptive and functional significance in human survival (Izard 1977; Plutchik 1980). Emotions can elicit action tendencies or states of readiness (Fridja 1986) as well as different assessments or appraisals of the environment (Lazarus 1984, 1991; Smith and Ellsworth 1985). The studies that follow examined whether the ERC phenomenon held for two commonly experienced negative emotions—sadness and fear/anxiety—and two pervasive positive emotions—amusement and contentment. The first study in this research

47

examined amusement and sadness; the second, contentment and fear/anxiety. A description of these emotions follows next.

Amusement/Joy

Amusement is often used interchangeably with happiness (Lazarus, 1991) and is a high-arousal positive emotion. Amusement results in an appraisal of safety and familiarity (Izard 1977). According to Frijda (1986), the action tendency associated with amusement and happiness is free *activation*. Amusement often creates the urge to be playful, whether it be physical, social, intellectual or artistic play. Fredrickson (1998, 2001) proposed that along with other positive emotions, amusement can broaden an individual's thought-action repertoire as well as build an individual's physical, intellectual, and social skills. These resources can be drawn on later, long after the experience of amusement has subsided. Additionally, amusement has recuperative powers and can serve as a remedy to stress (Tomkins 1962) and sustain coping ability in taxing situations (Lazarus, Kanner and Folkman 1980).

Sadness

Sadness, in constrast, is a low-arousal emotion and can slow the cognitive and motor systems. In one study, mothers' facial and vocal expression of sadness during face-to-face mother-child interactions increased expressions of sadnss and significantly decreased exploratory behavior in 9 month-old infants (Termine and Izard 1988). The slowing of cognitive processes associated with sadness may have adaptive significance in that individuals may engage in more careful reflection on disappointing performances and failures. This refection may help individuals gain new perspective (Izard and Ackerman 2000). Sadness results in an appraisal of trouble or loss (Tomkins

48

1963). It may also instigate prosocial behavior if it is not too intense (Manucia, Baumann and Cialdini 1984).

Contentment

Contentment is often used interchangeably with tranquility and serenity. It is a low-arousal positive emotion (Ellsworth and Smith 1988). An appraisal of safety along with a high degree of certainty and a low degree of effort is concomitant to contentment. Some have linked contentment with inactivity (Ellsworth and Smith 1988; Lazarus (1991); however, theoretical writings on contentment suggests that it prompts individuals to savor their current life circumstances, experience oneness with the world around them and incorporate recent events and achievements into their self-concept and outlook (Csikszentmihalyi 1990; deRivera *et al.*, 1989; Izard 1977). Fredrickson (1998, 2001) also characterized contentment as an emotion that broadens individuals' momentary thought-action repertoires and builds personal resources.

Fear/Anxiety

Fear and anxiety (anxiousness) are two affective states that are virtually inextricably linked. An important difference between the two concepts is that anxiety is often prestimulus (anticipatory to threatening stimuli) whereas as fear is poststimulus (elicited by a defined fear stimulus). Further, fear and is related to coping behavior, particularly escape and avoidance (Ohman 2000). It is an unpleasant affective state characterized by uneasiness and uncertainty and demands extreme amounts of effort (Izard 1977; Smith and Ellsworth 1985). Fear supports the action of flight (Fridja 1986).

When coping attempts fail, fear develops into anxiety (Epstein 1972). Anxiety is characterized by anticipation of future danger or misfortune, which is accompanied by a

49

feeling of "dysphoria or somatic symptoms of tension" (American Psychiatric Association 2000, p.820). Anxiety is an unresolved fear or a state of undirected arousal.

This research proposes that these four emotions play key roles in the ERC phenomenon. Three experiments were conducted to test these propositions. A description of procedures and measures used follows next.

STUDY 1

The purpose of this experiment was to determine whether individuals that were experiencing a negative emotion (sadness) were more likely to engage in the purchase of hedonic goods than those experiencing a positive emotion (amusement). Additionally, this study helped to determine whether emotion regulation strategy moderated the effect of emotions on hedonic consumption. Hypotheses 1 and 2 were tested with a 3 (emotions: amusement, neutral and sadness) X 2 (cognitive reappraisal: low/high) design. Two between-subject studies were performed using two different sets of products (Study1a and Study1b).

Hypothesis 1 predicted that individuals experiencing negative emotions would express more favorable attitudes, higher purchase intentions and willingness to pay a higher price for a hedonic product than individuals experiencing positive emotions. Further, Hypothesis 2 predicted that emotion regulation strategy would moderate the effect of emotions on attitudes, purchase intention and price. Specifically, low cognitive reappraisers would express more favorable attitudes, higher purchase intentions and willingness to pay a higher price for a hedonic product (see Figure 1) than high cognitive reappraisers.

50

In order to test Hypotheses 1 and 2, college students from a university in the southern part of the United States were randomly assigned to three different emotion conditions: amusement, neutral, and sadness. They were asked to watch a film that elicited one of these emotions. Using films to induce emotions has been used by a number of researchers in the behavioral literature (Rottenberg and Gross in press; Fredrickson *et al.* 2000; Garg, Wansink and Inman 2007). Films provide both visual and audio elements that help in altering subjective affective states and allow for focusing on discrete affective states versus global affect (Garg, Wansink and Inamn 2007).

Cognitive Reappraisal was a nonmanipulated, measured variable. Following the film, participants were asked to evaluate two products—one hedonic and one utilitarian in nature (Raghunathan and Corfman 2004).

Pilot Test 1

In order to ensure that the emotion-eliciting films produced the intended effect, and to test the reliability of measured variables, a pilot study was conducted. In this study, a sample consisting of 59 university students were shown film clips that were selected to elicit one of three emotions: amusement, sadness and a neutral or control condition. These films have been used previously in the literature (Rottenberg and Gross 2007).

The amusement film clip was an excerpt from one of the acts of stand-up comedian, Robin Williams (2002). The sadness film clip was taken from the movie *The Champ* (1979). The clip involves a scene where a little boy (Rick Schroder) sees his father (Jon Voight), a professional boxer, die after a boxing match. The neutral clip, entitled *Sticks,* was a noncommercial screensaver (Fredrickson *et al.* 2000). The neutral

51

condition was included as a control condition versus a no-film condition. Having a no-film condition, or having subjects do nothing, might confound emotional content, especially since participants might vary in basic cognitive demands. The neutral film was included with the intention of holding cognitive demands constant (Fredrickson and Levenson 1998; Fredrickson *et al.* 2000).

Following the films, subjects were given two purchase tasks, one of which was more hedonic in nature (going shopping for a new jacket to wear out with friends on the weekend) and the other more utilitarian in nature (purchasing a study packet for an upcoming exam). They were told that they would have to perform the two tasks within the next week, but were asked to select which they would prefer to do first. Following the preference/choice task, subjects were asked how deserving of their time versus how pleasurable each task would be. The participants were then given Gross and John's (2003) Emotion Regulation Questionnaire, which measures cognitive reappraisal. Items used to represent cognitive reappraisal included "When I want to feel less negative emotion (such as sadness or anger), I change what I'm thinking about" and "When I'm faced with a stressful situation, I make myself think about it in a way that helps me stay calm." Finally, subjects were given an Emotion Report Form (Eckman, Friesen and Ancoli 1980), which asked them to rate on a 9-point scale, (anchored by "I do not feel the emotion then slightest bit and "I feel this emotion very strongly") how they felt while viewing the film (e.g., "I feel sad," "I feel amused").

In order to test whether the content of the movies was successful in inducing the intended emotions, an analysis of variance was performed on the Emotion Report Form measures. There were main effects for both amusement, $F_{(2,54)}=16.76$, $p<.01$, and sadness, $F(2,55)=49.74$, $p<.05$. Planned contrasts confirmed that the amusement condition elicited significantly more amusement ($M=6.9$) than the sadness and neutral conditions ($M=3.05$ and $M=3.48$, $p<.001$). Similarly, the sadness condition elicited significantly more sadness ($M=6.15$) than the amusement and neutral conditions ($M=1.2$ and $M=1.68$, $p<.001$). The modal emotion report for the neutral condition (*Sticks*) was 1, which confirmed the emotional neutrality of this condition (Fredrickson *et al.* 2000).

Results from the preference/choice task indicate that going shopping for a jacket was viewed as more pleasurable than purchasing a study packet for a test ($M=5.67$ and $M=2.43$, $t(57) = 10.38$, $p<.001$). However, studying for a test was seen as more deserving of one's time than going shopping ($M=5.9$ and $M=4.6$, $t(57) = 4.21$, $p<.001$). Results show that there was a main effect for emotions on task preference order, $F(2,54) = 3.44$, $p<.05$. With higher numbers representing preference for the more hedonic task, planned contrasts suggest that individuals in the sad condition were more interested in engaging in the hedonic task first, which involved going shopping for a new jacket, than those in the amusement condition ($M=4.57$ and $M=3.02$, $p<.05$). Subjects in the sad condition also expressed greater interest in performing the hedonic task first than those in the neutral condition ($M=4.57$ and $M=3.49$, $p<.05$). Cognitive reappraisal demonstrated adequate reliability. Cronbach's alpha was .75.

Results from this pilot study provide preliminary evidence for the ERC phenomenon. Sad subjects were more likely than amused subjects to prefer performing a hedonic-oriented task first. Study 1 examined ERC further by assessing attitudes, purchase intentions as well as the price willing to pay for a hedonic good versus a utilitarian good. Cognitive reappraisal was examined for its moderating role in ERC.

Procedure

Participants in Study 1a were 167 undergraduate students at a southern university in the United States; likewise, Study 1b included 159 undergraduate students at the same university. Subjects were randomly assigned to 3 emotion conditions: amusement, sadness and a neutral or control condition. Subjects viewed the films used in the first pilot study: *Robin Williams*, *The Champ* and *Sticks*. They were given instructions to pay very close attention to the film and to make every attempt to envision that they were experiencing first-hand what was happening in the film.

After viewing the film, subjects were presented with one of two scenarios. In one of the scenarios, they were asked to imagine that they were at a silent auction and had an opportunity to bid on either a $35 gift certificate for groceries or a $35 gift certificate for dinner at a restaurant (Study 1a). This scenario was adapted from Okada (2005). The $35 gift certificate for dinner represented the hedonic good, and the $35 gift certificate for the groceries, the utilitarian good.[2] Individuals evaluated their attitude toward the product (selecting between which they felt more favorably), purchase intentions and the price they would be willing to pay for their item of preference. Next, individuals were given the Emotion Regulation Questionnaire (Gross and John 2003). The other scenario was a silent auction as well; however subjects were given the opportunity to bid on and evaluate a gift certificate for an automotive oil change versus a gift certificate for online music downloads (Study 1b). Both products were valued at $35.

---

[2] Results from a pretest including 36 respondents using Voss, Spangenberg and Grohmann (2003) Hedonic/Utilitarian Scale confirmed that a gift certificate for dinner was viewed as more hedonic (M=5.62 and 4.03, p<.001; measured on a 7-point scale) than a gift certificate for groceries and a gift certificate for groceries was viewed as more utilitarian (M=6.12 and 5.28, p<.001) than a gift certificate for dinner. Furthermore, an Ipod was considered more hedonic (M=5.47 and 3.41, p<.001) than a set of oil changes which was considered more utilitarian than an Ipod (M=6.15 and 4.81, p<.001).

Measurements

Independent Variables Manipulation Checks and Covariates

To ensure that the films viewed were successful in inducing the appropriate emotion, subjects were given the same Emotion Report Form administered in the first pretest. Again, they were asked to rate how they felt, on a 9-point t scale, while watching the film (*e.g.,* "I feel sad"). To assess the effectiveness of the manipulation, analysis of variance was conducted on the Emotion Report measures and the emotion conditions.

Emotion regulation strategy was a measured independent variable. In pretests, cognitive reappraisal (.73-.75) had proven to be reliable. Additionally, gender and affect intensity were used as covariates. Affect intensity, or the magnitude in which individuals respond to emotional stimuli (Larsen 1984; Larsen Diener1987), may have some effect on the extent to which subjects responded to emotion-inducing stimuli. Research has shown that females tend to exhibit higher levels of affect intensity than males (Fujita, Diener and Sandvik 1991). Affect intensity demonstrated sufficient reliability (.71) in pretests.

Dependent Variables

Participants evaluated how either the gift certificate for groceries and the gift certificate for dinner to a restaurant, or the music downloading and oil change appealed to them. An individual's attitude towards these products was measured with a modified version of an instrument that has been used previously in the literature (Stafford and Day 1995; Wansink and Ray 1992). Specifically, subjects were asked to evaluate on a 7-point scale whether one of the products sounded "good," "desirable," "appealing," or

55

"favorable," at the present moment. The scale was anchored by "The *gift certificate for groceries* sounds..." and" The *gift certificate for dinner* sounds..." etc. This instrument demonstrated acceptable reliability (.89).

Next, participants reported the extent to which they were inclined to purchase the product. A modified version of a purchase intention measure used extensively in the literature (Bearden 1985; Stafford 1996; Taylor, Miracle and Wilson 1997) was used to represent this construct. Subjects responded to a 7-point scale (anchored by "strongly disagree" and "strongly agree") with five items regarding whether their purchase of one of the items was "likely," "probable," "certain," "possible" or "definite." Reliability for this instrument was .96.

Finally, participants were given the opportunity to bid (with actual money) on both the products. Those individuals with the highest bids received the respective product.

STUDY 2

Baumeister (2002) proposed that individuals experiencing negative emotions might show an increase in the consumption of hedonic products such as snack foods, music CDs or flashy clothes. Additionally, when various demands deplete an individual's resources, individuals may fail at self-regulation (Muraven and Baumeister 2000). When individuals fail at self-regulation, they may be more prone to engaging in consumption of an impulsive nature to achieve gratification in the short-term (Vohs and Faber 2002). The purpose of this experiment was to ascertain whether emotions, ego depletion and emotion regulation strategy had an effect on impulsive hedonic purchase behavior.

Study 2 tested study hypotheses 3-7. These hypotheses were tested with a 2 (ego depletion: present/absent) X 3 (emotion: contentment/neutrality/fear and anxiety) X 2 (cognitive reappraisers: low/high) between-subjects design. Hypothesis 3 predicted that ego depletion would influence individuals in such a way that these individuals would exhibit greater levels of buying impulsiveness for a hedonic good than individuals that had not been subjected to an ego depletion task. Additionally, hypothesis 4 proposed that individuals that had been subjected to an ego depletion task would exhibit more favorable attitudes, greater desirability and higher purchase intentions for a hedonic purchase than individuals that had not been subjected to an ego depletion task.

Hypothesis 5 predicted an interaction between ego depletion and emotions. Specifically, individuals that had been subjected to an ego depletion task and were experiencing negative emotion or were in a neutral affective state would report more favorable attitudes, greater desirability and higher purchase intentions than individuals that had not been subjected to an ego depletion task and were experiencing negative emotion or were in a neutral affective state. However, it was predicted that there would be no differences between individuals experiencing positive emotion in both the ego depletion condition and the no-ego depletion condition. Further, hypothesis 6 predicted that low cognitive reappraisers that were subjected to an ego depletion task and were experiencing negative emotions would exhibit more favorable attitudes, greater desirability and higher purchase intentions than individuals that were high cognitive reappraisers and had been subjected to an ego depletion task and were experiencing negative emotions. Similarly, hypothesis 6 predicted that low cognitive reappraisers that were subjected to an ego depletion task and were experiencing positive emotions would exhibit more favorable attitudes, greater desirability and higher purchase intentions than their high cognitive reappraiser counterparts. It was also predicted that there would be no differences between low and high cognitive reappraisers and ego depleted individuals in the neutral affective state. Finally, hypothesis 7 proposed that there would be significant differences in levels of buying impulsiveness for a hedonic good between low and high cognitive reappraisers. It was hypothesized that low cognitive reappraisers would demonstrate higher levels of buying impulsiveness.

Pilot Tests 2 and 3

To ensure that the emotion induction and the ego depletion task worked as anticipated, a pilot tests were conducted. Pilot test 2 tested whether the emotion induction for contentment and fear/anxiety worked. A sample consisting of 62 university students were shown film clips that elicited one of three emotions: contentment, fear/anxiety and a neutral or control condition. These films had also been used previously in the behavioral literature (Rottenberg and Gross 2007). The contentment film clip was taken from *Alaska's Wild Denali*, a nature/promotional film for Alaska. The fear/anxiety film clip was an excerpt from *Silence of the Lambs*, where an FBI agent chases after an alleged murderer in an old house. The same neutral clip used in the first pilot test, *Sticks,* was used for the neutral, or control condition.

Similar to the first pretest, after viewing the films, subjects were given two purchase tasks, one of which was more hedonic in nature (going out with friends for an enjoyable time and grabbing a bite to eat), and the other more utilitarian in nature (calling the plumber out to fix a broken sink). These tasks were adapted from Raghunathan and Corfman 2004. Just as in the first pilot test, participants were told that they would have

58

to perform the two tasks within the next week, but were given the option of selecting which they would prefer to do first. Following the preference/choice task, subjects rated how deserving of their time versus how pleasurable they perceived each task to be. Subjects were then given the Emotion Report Form (Eckman, Friesen and Ancoli 1980), which asked them to rate how they felt while viewing the film.

In order to test whether the content of the movies was successful in inducing the desired emotions, an analysis of variance was performed on the Emotion Report Form measures, and there were main effects for both contentment, $F(2,56)=29.78$, $p<.001$ and fear/anxiety, $F(2,56)=73.14$, $p<.001$. Planned contrasts confirmed that the contentment condition elicited significantly more contentment ($M=6.13$) than the fear/anxiety condition ($M=1.81$, $p<.001$)) and the neutral condition ($M=4.36$, $p<.05$). Similarly, the fear/anxiety condition elicited significantly more fear/anxiety ($M=6.5$) than the contentment and neutral conditions ($M=1.7$ and $M=1.4$, $p<.001$). The modal emotion report for the neutral condition (*Sticks*) was 2, indicating the emotional neutrality of the video clip (Fredrickson *et al.* 2000).

Results from the preference/choice task indicated that going out with friends was viewed as more pleasurable than meeting with the plumber ($M=6.2$ and $M=2.19$, $t(61)=15.94$, $p<.001$). However, meeting with the plumber was not seen as more deserving of one's time than going out with friends ($M=5.54$ and $M=6.0$, $t(61)=1.99$, $p>.05$). Results also indicate that there was a main effect for emotions on task preference order, $F(2,56)=3.97$, $p<.05$. Individuals in the fear/anxiety condition were more interested in engaging in the hedonic task first, going out with friends, than those in the contentment condition ($M=6.6$ and $M=5.01$, $p<.05$). Subjects in the fear/anxiety

59

condition also expressed greater interest in performing the hedonic task first than those in the neutral condition (M=6.6 and M=4.56, p<.05).

This pretest helped to validate the manipulation to be used in the subsequent study as well as provided preliminary evidence for the ERC phenomenon with the discrete emotions, fear/anxiety and contentment.

Pretest 3 was conducted to confirm that the ego depletion manipulation (adapted from Baumeister *et al*. 1998) to be used in study 2 would have the intended effect. One-hundred thirty-eight undergraduate students from a southern university were assigned to one of two conditions: an ego depletion condition or control condition. The control condition involved crossing out all instances of the letter "e" in a typewritten paragraph from an upper-level college statistics text book. This was used as the control condition because people can learn to do this easily and quickly, becoming accustomed to scanning for every "e" and then crossing it out. The ego depletion task, however, was more difficult. Subjects were told not to cross out the letter "e" if a vowel was adjacent to it or if the "e" was one letter away from a vowel. In addition, the resolution of the text was denigrated to make the task more difficult. This task would presumably aid in depleting the ego because subjects would scan for each "e," but would then have to override the response of crossing it out whenever any of the criteria just delineated were met. As a manipulation check (which appeared at the end of the survey), subjects were asked to rate on a 7-point scale how difficult the task was, how much effort it required and how much they had to concentrate in order to complete the task.

Following the manipulation, participants in both conditions were presented with a scenario where they were asked to imagine that they were in the grocery store and came

60

upon a delicious-looking cheesecake in the bakery section. They were asked about their attitude toward the cheesecake, desire for the cheesecake as well as their likelihood of purchasing a piece of the cheesecake. The degree to which a subject liked cheesecake was used as a covariate.

Results from the manipulation check indicated that subjects assigned to the ego depletion condition rated their task more difficult, $M=3.6$ and $M=2.4$, $t(129)=4.76$ $p<.001$, and also reported that it required more concentration than the control group, $M=4.9$ and $M=3.44$, $t(129)=5.11$, $p<.001$; thus, the ego depletion task had the intended effect. Further, results showed that individuals in the ego depletion condition where less likely to resist the tempting cheesecake and expressed higher purchase intentions for it than the control group, $M=4.6$ and $M=3.9$, $t(110)=2.55$, $p<.05$. However, there were no significant differences between the ego depletion condition and the control condition for attitude towards the cheesecake, $M=2.14$ and $M=2.71$, $t(111)=1.81$, $p>.05$.

Procedure

Participants in Study 2 were 226 college students from a southern university in the United States. Subjects were randomly assigned to an ego depletion condition or a control condition. The ego depletion task administered in Pretest 3 was given to the participants. Following this, subjects viewed a film that elicited one of the three emotions: contentment, fear/anxiety and a neutral or control condition. The films used in Pretest 2 to induce these emotions were used in this study.[3]

Next, subjects were presented with a shopping situation adapted from Rook and Fisher (1995), which involved the use of an imaginary stimulus situation. The scenario follows:

---

[3] The sequence of these manipulations were reversed, or counterbalanced, to avert any order effects.

Imagine you are a college student with a part-time job. In three-days, you will get your paycheck, but until then you only have $20 left for necessities. You go to Lagasse's Market to buy some needed groceries and see a display for a decadent bakery-style cheesecake. The cheesecake costs $12 dollars and would be great to share with friends.

Following this, participants evaluated their attitude, desirability and purchase intentions toward the cheesecake. Additionally, their degree of impulsivity was measured. The Emotion Regulation Questionnaire (Gross and John 2003), measuring the cognitive reappraisal was also administered.

Measurements

Independent Variables Manipulation Checks and Covariates

To ensure that the films viewed were successful in inducing the appropriate emotion, subjects were given the same Emotion Report Form used previously. To test whether ego depletion was successfully manipulated, subjects were asked to rate on a 7-point Likert scale whether the task of crossing out the letter "e" was difficult and required effort.

Covariates used in the analysis were gender, a subject's like/dislike of cheesecake, likelihood to eat to manage emotions and impulsivity. Likelihood to eat to manage emotions was measured using three items, "I eat to cheer myself up when I am feeling bad," "When I am feeling bad, I eat something," "Eating something helps me to cope with feeling bad." Coefficient alpha for the scale was .95. Also, since level of impulsiveness was assessed as a dependent variable, inherent differences in levels of impulsivity was accounted for by including Puri's (1996) Consumer Impulsiveness Scale (CIS). This scale demonstrated sufficient reliability (.77) in pretests.

Dependent Variables

Similar to Study 1, attitudes toward the product and purchase intentions was measured. Attitude toward the cheesecake was measured using six semantic differential items: "A slice of cheesecake sounds good/bad, tasteful/not tasteful at the present moment. Reliability for this measure was .98. Likewise, purchase intentions was measured using six items: "The probability that I will purchase the cheesecake is likely/unlikely, probable/not probable.." This scale also demonstrated acceptable reliability. Cronbach's Alpha was .89.

In addition to attitudes and purchase intentions, desirability was measured because desire is characterized by cravings or urgings that are motivational in nature and often antecedent to impulsive behavior (Dhoakia, Gopinath and Bagozzi 2005). The experience of desires is quite common in everyday life, such as when a shopper prepares a list of items to purchase at the market, but when confronted with a tantalizing unplanned purchase option, concedes. Desirability was measured by asking subjects whether they had a "craving, urge or longing for the cheesecake." Reliability for the desirability measure was .95.

Finally, level of buying impulsiveness was measured using an instrument taken from Rook and Fisher (1995). Subjects were instructed to select from which of the following purchase alternatives they would make: 1) buy needed staple groceries only 2) want the cheesecake but not buy it 3) decide not to buy all the staple groceries needed to have money for the cheesecake 4) buy both the groceries needed and the cheesecake with a credit card 5) buy all the groceries needed, cheesecake, and some strawberry topping for

63

the cheesecake with a credit card. Each choice alternative represented a higher level, or degree, of buying impulsiveness.

STUDY 3

The final study in this research assessed actual behavior for impulsive and hedonic consumption. Subjects were presented with a purchase decision task after being exposed to ego depletion and emotion-inducing stimuli. The purchase decision task included allowing subjects to exchange a dollar that they were given at the inception of the study (as a gift for participating) for a characteristically hedonic product (two chocolate chip cookies) versus a characteristically utilitarian product (a fruit pack consisting of an apple and banana). The purpose of the study was to evaluate how ego depletion, emotions and emotion regulation strategy effect actual impulsive and hedonic consumption. Study 3 was a 2 (ego depletion: present/absent) X 3 (amusement/neutral/ sadness) X 2 (cognitive reappraisal: low/high) between-subjects design.

Pilot Test 4

Because a new ego depletion manipulation was used for Study 3, a pretest was conducted to ensure that the would work and to also test for impulsivity in purchasing behavior. Forty-five undergraduate students from a southern university were assigned to an ego depletion condition and a control condition. The ego depletion condition was a thought suppression task where individuals in the ego depletion condition were told to list their thoughts on a sheet of paper, but to refrain from thinking about a white bear (Wegner 1989; Vohs and Faber 2007). Individuals in the control condition were simply given instruction to list their thoughts.

Following the ego depletion task, individuals were presented with a scenario where they were told that they were out walking and found two dollars on the street. They were also told that shortly after finding the two dollars, they came upon a snack food stand and had the option of purchasing an array of products. These products included a granola bar, a chocolate bar, orange juice, a coke, pretzels, Doritos, a bagel and a donut (Vohs and Faber 2007). The items were priced between $.75 and $1.25. Subjects could choose to buy as much as they liked.

As a manipulation check for ego depletion, individuals were asked how worn-out they were. Subjects in the ego depletion condition indicated that they were more worn-out (M=5.52 and 4.52, $t(38)$=1.92, $p<.05$) than individuals in the no-ego depletion condition. Results also indicated that individuals in the ego depletion condition expressed greater impulsive purchasing intent. Ego-depleted individuals bought more than non-ego depleted individuals (M=2.0 and 1.68, $t(38)$=1.77, $p<.05$) and also spent more money (M=2.07 and 1.68, $t=(38)$=2.0, $p<.05$).

Procedure

In Study 3, two hundred and thirteen subjects were first presented with the ego depletion task. Following this, they viewed films to induce amusement and sadness (*Robin Williams, Sticks* and *The Champ*—used in Study 1). Subjects were then presented with the purchasing situation where they were given the option to buy cookies or fruit for a $1. Subjects were allowed to purchase as many of the products as they desired.

It was predicted that more participants in the ego depletion task would purchase the products than in the no-ego depletion task. Additionally, it was expected that more individuals in the ego depletion and sadness condition would choose the hedonic product

65

(cookies) than individuals in the ego depletion and amusement condition. Further, it was anticipated that more individuals in the ego depletion and amusement condition would choose the fruit pack than individuals in the ego depletion and sadness condition. Finally, it was proposed that low cognitive reappraisers in the ego depletion and sadness condition would select the hedonic product more than high cognitive reappraisers in the ego depletion task and sadness condition.

In the next chapter, results from the three studies discussed are presented. Descriptive and multivariate methods were used as analytical approaches for ascertaining relationships between variables and differences in main and interacting effects.

CHAPTER 4

Results

STUDY 1 RESULTS

The first study hypothesis examined whether individuals experiencing a negative emotion (sadness), are more likely to express favorable attitudes, greater purchase intentions and willingness to pay a higher price for a hedonic good than those experiencing a positive emotion (amusement). The second hypothesis in Study 1 tested the moderating role of cognitive reappraisal on emotions for attitude, purchase intentions, and price. Hypotheses 1 and 2 were tested with a 3 (emotions: amusement/neutral/sadness) X 2 (cognitive reappraisal: low/high) between-subjects design. These hypotheses were tested with two sets of products in two between-subjects designs. In each set, one product was more utilitarian in nature, while the other more hedonic. One set of products was a gift certificate for groceries (utilitarian) and a gift certificate for dinner at a restaurant (hedonic), while the other set of products was a gift certificate for an oil change (utilitarian) and a gift certificate for online music downloading (hedonic). Results are reported first for the set of products that included the gift certificate for groceries and the gift certificate for dinner first.

Study 1a: Gift Certificate for Groceries versus Gift Certificate for Dinner
Manipulation Check

Manipulation checks were performed to make certain that the emotion-eliciting films were successful in inducing the intended emotions. Similar to the pretests, subjects were given the Emotion Report Form (Eckman, Friesen and Ancoli 1980), which asked them to rate on a 9-point scale (anchored by "I do not feel the emotion the slightest bit and "I feel this emotion very strongly") how they felt while viewing the film (e.g., "I feel sad," " I feel amused"). An analysis of variance on the Emotion Report Form measures

68

revealed a main effect for both amusement, $F(2, 163)=97$, $p<.01$ and sadness $F(2,164)=206.1$, $p<.01$. Planned contrasts confirmed that the amusement condition elicited significantly more amusement ($M=6.8$) than the sadness and neutral conditions ($M=2.6$ and $M=3.4$, $p<.01$). Correspondingly, the sadness condition elicited significantly more sadness ($M=6.7$) than the amusement and neutral conditions ($M=1.5$ and $M=1.7$, $p<.01$). The modal emotion report for the neutral condition (*Sticks*) was 2, which confirmed the emotional neutrality of this condition.

Covariates

Gender and affect intensity were used as covariates in this study. An analysis of covariance was performed to test hypotheses 1 and 2. When performing an ANCOVA, covariates should not be correlated or interact with independent measures (Hair *et al.* 2006). To ensure that these assumptions were not violated, correlations were obtained on covariates and independent variables. Additionally, a median split was performed on the continuous covariate, affect intensity. For each dependent measure, an ANOVA was performed on the covariates and the independent variables to assess any potential interactions between the covariates and the independent variables.

Results from the correlations reveal no significant relationships among emotion, gender and affect intensity ($p>.05$). Also, no significant relationships were found between cognitive reappraisal and affect intensity. However, a significant relationship was found between cognitive reappraisal and gender ($r = .18$, $p<.05$). Analysis of variance on the covariates and independent measures for each dependent measure indicated no significant interactions ($p>.05$).

Test of H1

Hypothesis 1a-c predicted that individuals experiencing a negative emotion (sadness) would express more favorable attitudes, higher purchase intentions and willingness to pay a higher price for a hedonic product than individuals experiencing a positive emotion (amusement). Further, Hypothesis 2 predicted that cognitive reappraisal would moderate the effect of emotions on attitudes, purchase intention and price willing to pay. Specifically, low cognitive reappraisers would express more favorable attitudes, higher purchase intentions and willingness to pay a higher price for a hedonic product than high cognitive reappraisers. To test these hypotheses, an ANCOVA was performed. The outcome of the ANCOVA is presented in Table 1.

Univariate follow-up tests indicated a main effect for attitudes towards the product (p<.05). With high numbers indicating more favorable attitudes for the hedonic product, subjects in the sad condition expressed the most favorable attitudes toward the hedonic product (M= 5.2), following those in the amusement condition (M =5.13) and finally, the neutral condition (M= 4.57). However, even though the direction of the means were consistent with hypothesis 1, simple contrasts revealed significant differences between the neutral and sad condition (p<.05) and the neutral and amusement condition (p<.05) only. Hence, hypothesis 1a was not fully supported. Additionally, there was a main effect for purchase intentions (p<.05), which was qualified by a significant interaction. Subjects in the sad condition expressed greater purchase intentions for the hedonic good over the utilitarian good (M= 4.91). Both the amusement and neutral conditions followed in preference for the hedonic good (M= 4.7 and M= 4.03). However, the only significant statistical differences existed between the neutral

70

and sadness conditions. Hypothesis 1b was not supported. Means are presented in Table 2.

Further, hypothesis 1c predicted that subjects in the sad condition would pay a higher price for the hedonic good than subjects in the amusement condition. Results show that means were in the opposite direction than predicted. Individuals in the neutral condition ($M = 20.79$) appeared to be the least price sensitive to the hedonic product, followed by those in the positive condition ($M = 18.41$) and then the sad condition ($M=16.34$). However, none of these differences reached statistical significance. Hypothesis 1c was not supported.

Test of H2

Hypothesis 2a-c predicted that cognitive reappraisal would moderate the effect of emotions on attitudes toward the product, purchase intentions and price willing to pay. Low cognitive reappraisers in the sad condition would express greater affinity for the hedonic product than high cognitive reappraisers in the sad condition. Results indicated a marginally significant interaction between emotions and cognitive reappraisal ($p<.10$). For attitude towards the product, low cognitive reappraisers expressed more favorable attitudes toward the hedonic product than high cognitive reappraisers ($M = 5.32$ and $M = 5.17$). These differences did not reach statistical significance ($p>.05$). However, for purchase intentions in the sadness condition, low cognitive reappraisers expressed significantly greater purchase intentions than high cognitive reappraisers ($M = 5.25$ and $M= 4.58$, $t(57)= 1.8$, $p<.05$). Hence, hypothesis 2a was not supported, but hypothesis 2b was supported (see Figure 4).

Finally, hypothesis 2c predicted that low cognitive reappraisers in the sad condition would be willing to pay a higher price for the hedonic good than high cognitive reappraisers. The means were consistent with hypothesis 2c. Low cognitive reappraisers in the sad condition were willing to pay a higher price for the hedonic good than high cognitive reappraisers (M =18.6 and M = 14.3). However, these means did not reach statistical significance (p>.05).

Next, results are presented for the products, which included a gift certificate for an oil change and online music downloading

Study 1b: Gift Certificate for Oil Change versus Online Music Downloading

Manipulation Check

Similar to the first set of products, manipulation checks were performed to test the efficacy of the emotion-eliciting films. An analysis of variance on the Emotion Report Form measures revealed a main effect for both amusement, $F(2, 149)=88.84$, p<.01 and sadness $F(2,150)=244.25$, p<.01. Planned contrasts confirmed that the amusement condition elicited significantly more amusement (M=7.02) than the sadness and neutral conditions (M=2.28 and M=4.0, p<.01). Similarly, the sadness condition elicited significantly more sadness (M=6.7) than the amusement and neutral conditions (M=1.45 and M=1.3, p<.01). The modal emotion report for the neutral condition (*Sticks*) was 2, which confirmed the emotional neutrality of this condition.

Covariates

An ANOVA performed on the covariates and the independent variables revealed only a significant interaction between gender and emotions (p<.05). Results from the correlations obtained indicated no significant relationships among emotion, gender and affect intensity (p>.05). Also, no significant relationships among cognitive reappraisal, gender and affect intensity (p>.05) were found.

Test of H1

To test hypotheses for the second set of products, an ANCOVA was performed (see Table 3). Univariate follow-up tests indicated that there was no main effect for attitude towards the product and purchase intentions. For price willing to pay for the product, means did reach statistical significance, but once again were in the opposite direction from what was predicted. Individuals in the amusement condition ($M = 13.31$) appeared to be the least price sensitive to the hedonic product, followed by those in the sadness condition ($M = 6.87$) and then the neutral condition ($M=6.56$). Hypothesis 1a-c were not supported. Means are presented in Table 4.

Test of H2

Again, hypothesis 2a-c predicted that cognitive reappraisal would moderate the effect of emotions on attitudes toward the product, purchase intentions and price willing to pay. Results indicated that there was no significant interaction between emotions and cognitive reappraisal for attitude towards the product, purchase intentions and price willing to pay. Hence, hypotheses 2a-c were not supported.

STUDY 2 RESULTS

The second study of this research tested hypotheses 3-7. These hypotheses were tested with a 3 (emotion: contentment/neutrality/fear and anxiety) X 2 (ego depletion: present/absent) X 2 (cognitive reappraisers: low/high) between-subjects design. In this study, subjects were first exposed to an ego depletion task where they were instructed to cross out the letter "e" only if it did not meet certain criteria in a paragraph of text that was difficult to read.[4] However, subjects in a control condition were given much simpler instructions and the text in the paragraph was much clearer and easier to read. Following the ego depletion task, participants were randomly assigned to a condition where they were shown a film that elicited either contentment, fear/anxiety or no emotion (control condition). Subjects were then presented with a scenario where they reported their attitudes, desire, level of buying impulsiveness and purchase likelihood for cheesecake.

Manipulation Check

As in Study 1, manipulation checks were performed to ensure that the emotion-eliciting films were successful in inducing the intended emotions. Using the Emotion Report Form (Eckman, Friesen and Ancoli 1980) as check measures, an analysis of variance revealed a main effect for contentment, $F(2, 218)=36.1$, $p<.01$ and fear/anxiety $F(2,218)=158.15$, $p<.01$. Planned contrasts showed that the contentment condition induced significantly more contentment ($M=5.65$) than the neutral and fear/anxiety conditions ($M=2.65$ and $M=3.29$, $p<.01$). Likewise, the fear/anxiety condition elicited more fear/anxiety ($M=5.38$) than the neutral and contentment conditions ($M=1.35$ and $M=1.28$, $p<.01$). The modal report for the neutral condition was 1 for all emotions, but 3 for the amusement condition.

Next, the ego depletion task in Study 2 involved crossing out the letter "e" based on various stipulations. Manipulation check items for this task asked subjects if performing the task was difficult and required effort and concentration. The scores from these three items were combined, and an analysis of variance yielded $F(1,218)=26.68$, $p<.01$ a main effect for ego depletion. Individuals in the ego depletion task rated their

---

[4] Counterbalancing the ego depletion task with the emotion-inducing stimuli yielded no significant differences.

task more difficult, and thus, requiring more effort and concentration (M=4.28) than the control condition (M=3.33, p<.01).

Covariates

Because an ANCOVA was performed to test hypotheses 3-7, an ANOVA was first run on each dependent measure along with the independent variables and covariates to ensure that there were no interactions between the independent variables and covariates. Median splits were performed on the covariates—impulsivity and whether an individual might eat to regulate their emotions or liked cheesecake. No significant interactions were found among these covariates and the independent variables, (p>.05).

Additionally, independent variables and covariates were checked for significant correlations. Results from the correlations revealed no significant relationships between independent variables and covariates, (p>.05).

Test of H3

An ANCOVA was performed to test H3-H7 (see Table 5). Hypothesis 3 predicted that ego depletion would influence individuals in such a way that ego depleted individuals would exhibit greater levels of buying impulsiveness for a hedonic good than non-ego depleted individuals. Univariate follow-up tests revealed no significant main effect for buying impulsiveness (*M*=1.41 and *M*=1.38). Hypothesis 4 was not supported.

Test of H4

Hypotheses 4a-c proposed that individuals subjected to an ego depletion task would exhibit more favorable attitudes, greater desirability and higher purchase intentions for a hedonic good than individuals not subjected to an ego depletion task. Results showed that there were no significant main effects for attitude towards the

75

cheesecake and desirability for the cheesecake. However, there was a marginally significant main effect for ego depletion for purchase intentions. Opposite of prediction, individuals in the no-ego depletion condition demonstrated higher purchase intentions for the hedonic good (cheesecake) than individuals in the ego depletion condition (M=3.19 and M=2.85, t(57)=1.98, p<.10). Hence, hypothesis 4 was not supported.

Test of H5

Hypotheses 5a-c examined the interactive effects of ego depletion and emotions. Specifically, it was predicted that emotions would interact with ego depletion so that ego depleted individuals in a negative or neutral emotion condition would report more favorable attitudes, greater desirability and higher purchase intentions than non-ego depleted individuals in a negative or neutral emotion condition. It was also predicted that there would be no differences between ego depleted and non-ego depleted individuals in the positive emotion condition. Results from planned contrasts indicated no significant differences between the ego and no-ego depletion conditions in the neutral (M=5.48 and M=5.59, p>.05) or fear/anxiety conditions (M=5.52 and M=5.2, p>.05) for attitude toward the cheesecake. Nonetheless, hypothesis 5a predicted no differences for attitudes between the ego and no-ego depletion condition for contentment and there were no significant differences, p>.05.

For desirability for the product, there was also no significant differences between the neutral and fear/anxiety conditions between ego depleted and non-ego depleted conditions (M=2.69 and M=2.81, p>.05; M=3.08 and M=3.29, p>.05). Additionally, as predicted in hypothesis 5, there were no differences in desirability between the ego and no-ego depletion condition for contentment, p>.05.

76

Results from hypothesis 5 revealed no significance differences between the neutral emotion and fear/anxiety conditions between ego depletion and no-ego depletion for purchase intentions (*M*=2.45 and *M*=2.41, p>.05) and (*M*=3.31 and *M*=3.6, p>.05). However, opposite of prediction, there was a marginally significant effect between ego depletion and no-ego depletion for the contentment condition (see Figure 5), with subjects in the no-ego depletion condition expressing stronger purchase intentions for the cheesecake than individuals in the ego depletion condition (*M*=3.57 and *M*=2.8, p<.10).

Test of H6

With regard to emotion regulation strategy, hypotheses 6a-c predicted that low cognitive reappraisers subjected to an ego depletion task experiencing negative emotions would exhibit more favorable attitudes, greater desirability and higher purchase intentions than high cognitive reappraisers for a hedonic good. Furthermore, no differences between low and high cognitive reappraisers for the ego depletion and neutral affective state were predicted.

Contrary to prediction, results for attitude toward the product showed that there are no significant differences between low cognitive reappraisers and high cognitive reappraisers (*M*=5.24 and *M*=5.47, p>.05) in the contentment condition. However, as anticipated, there were no significant differences between low and high reappraisers in the neutral condition (*M*=5.43 and *M*=5.54, p>.05) for attitude towards the product in the ego depletion condition. Finally, there were marginally significant differences between the fear/anxiety condition; however, means were in the opposite direction (see Figure 6). High cognitive reappraisers expressed more favorable attitudes toward the cheesecake

77

than low cognitive reappraisers (M=5.83 and M=5.22, t(38) = 1.92 p<.10) in the ego depletion condition.

For desirability, there were no significant differences between low and high cognitive reappraisers in the contentment condition (M=3.01 and M=2.81, p>.05)—even though means were in the appropriate direction. As predicted, there were no differences between low and high cognitive reappraisers in the neutral condition. Finally, in the fear/anxiety condition for desirability, there were no significance differences (M=2.98 and M=3.18, p>.05), differing from prediction.

Next, results from planned contrasts indicated that there were marginally significant differences between low and high cognitive reappraisers in the contentment condition for purchase intentions (M=3.1 and M=2.45, t(42)= 1.80, p<.10). As predicted, low cognitive reappraisers had higher purchase intentions for the cheesecake than high cognitive reappraisers (see Figure 7). Also, as expected, there are no significant differences between low and high cognitive reappraisers in the neutral condition for purchase intentions (M=2.4 and M=2.51, p>.10). The fear/anxiety condition, however, yielded no significant differences between low and high cognitive reappraisers (M=3.12 and M=3.51, p>.05).

Test of H7

The final hypothesis of Study 2, hypothesis 7, predicted that there would be significant differences in levels of buying impulsiveness for a hedonic good (cheesecake) between low and high cognitive reappraisers, with low reappraisers demonstrating higher levels of buying impulsiveness. This hypothesis was not supported. There were no significant differences between the low and high cognitive reappraisers in both the ego depletion and fear/anxiety conditions (M=1.43 and M=1.65, p>.05).

Other Findings

Additional results from Study 2 revealed a main effect for emotions. Individuals in the fear/anxiety condition expressed the highest purchase intentions for the cheesecake than any of the emotion conditions. There were significant differences between the fear/anxiety and neutral conditions (*M*=3.45 and *M*=2.43, p<.05). Additionally, there were significant differences between the contentment and neutral conditions for purchase intentions (*M*=3.18 and *M*=2.43, p<.05).

Other findings also indicate that there was a significant interaction between emotions and cognitive reappraisal. In the contentment condition, low cognitive reappraisers expressed more favorable purchase intentions for the cheesecake than high cognitive reappraisers (*M*=3.01 and *M*= 2.4, t(25)=2.0, p<.05).

A main effect was also found for attitudes and desirability for the cheesecake for individuals that reported that they characteristically eat when feeling bad. Specifically, individuals that indicated that they eat when feeling bad, or emotional eaters, had more favorable attitudes for the cheesecake than non-emotional eaters (*M*=6.02 and *M*=2.58, p<.01). Likewise, emotional eaters had higher levels of desirability for the cheesecake than non-emotional eaters (*M*=3.25 and *M*=1.48, p<.05).

STUDY 3 RESULTS

Study 3 in this research was conducted to examine how ego depletion, emotions and emotion regulation strategy would affect impulsive buying behavior for a hedonic product. The experiment was a 2 (ego depletion: present/absent) X 3 (amusement/neutral/ sadness) X 2 (cognitive reappraisal: low/high) between-subjects design. Subjects were all given a dollar for participating in the experiment. Next, they were given an ego depletion task that asked then them to list their thoughts, but to refrain from thinking about a white bear. Following this, they were randomly assigned to conditions where they viewed films that induced amusement and sadness (*Robin Williams and The Champ*). There was also neutral, or control condition (*Sticks*). Subjects were then presented with a purchasing situation where they were given the opportunity to buy two chocolate chip cookies or fruit (an apple and banana) for a $1.

Manipulation Checks

Once again, manipulation checks were performed to ensure that the emotion-eliciting films were successful in inducing the intended emotions. An analysis of variance revealed a main effect for amusement, $F(2, 210)=138.96$, $p<.01$ and sadness $F(2,210)=189.96$, $p<.01$. Planned contrasts showed that the amusement condition induced significantly more amusement ($M=7.49$) than the neutral and sadness conditions ($M=3.27$ and $M=2.72$, $p<.01$). Similarly, the sadness condition elicited more sadness ($M=6.4$) than the neutral and amusement conditions ($M=1.83$ and $M=1.54$, $p<.01$). The modal report for the neutral condition was 1 for sadness, but 2 for the amusement condition.

The manipulation check for ego depletion asked subjects how worn-out and tired they felt after the task. There was no main effect for ego depletion (p>.05). For individuals in the ego depletion condition, the mean score for tiredness was 3.26 for the ego depletion condition and 3.4 for those in the no-ego depletion condition. For how worn-out subjects were, means were 3.07 for individuals in the ego depletion condition and 3.05 for those in the no-ego depletion condition.

Test of Hypotheses

It was predicted that more participants in the ego depletion task would purchase one of the products than participants in the no-ego depletion. However, contrary to expectations, there were ten individuals in the no-ego depletion condition that purchased products and eight in the ego depletion condition (see Table 10 series).

It was also expected that more individuals in the ego depletion and negative emotion condition would choose the hedonic product (cookies) than individuals in the ego depletion and positive emotion condition. Results demonstrated that there was one person in the ego depletion and sadness condition that did purchase the cookies, but four individuals in the ego depletion and amusement condition purchased cookies.

Finally, it was predicted that low cognitive reappraisers in the ego depletion and negative emotion condition would select the hedonic product more than high cognitive reappraisers in the ego depletion and negative emotion condition. The data showed, however, that no low cognitive reappraisers in the ego depletion and sadness condition purchased any of the products, but one high cognitive reappraiser in the ego depletion and sadness condition purchased the cookies.

81

Other Findings

After being presented with the purchasing option, individuals were asked how tempted they were to buy "something," how tempted they were to buy the fruit, as well as how tempted they were to buy the cookies. Subjects in the amusement condition expressed the greatest temptation to buy something (M=3.94), which was significantly greater than subjects in the neutral and sadness conditions (M=2.88 and M=2.99, p<.05). There were also varying degrees of temptation for the fruit. For example, subjects in the amusement condition expressed greater temptation to purchase the fruit (M=3.51), than those in the neutral and sadness condition (M=2.97 and M=2.6, p<.05).

With regard to temptation for the cookies, individuals in the amusement condition once again, expressed the greatest temptation (M=3.38). Differences between the amusement and neutral condition (M=2.21) were significant, p<.05. Also, differences between the sadness (M=2.86) and neutral condition were significant, p<.05. There were no significant differences between the amusement and sadness conditions, however.

Results from Study 3 also revealed that individuals that scored high on impulsivity (as an individual difference) were more tempted to buy something (to buy the fruit and to buy the cookies) than individuals that scored lower on impulsivity, p<.05. Additionally, contrasts indicate that high impulsive individuals in the amusement condition were more tempted to buy something than low impulsive individuals (M=4.72 and M=3.33, p<.05). This also held for high impulsive individuals in the amusement condition for both temptation to purchase the fruit (M=4.0 and M=3.05, p<.05) and cookies (M=2.7 and M=1.75, p<.05).

FOLLOW-UP STUDY RESULTS

In an attempt to better ascertain the effect that ego depletion might have on impulsive behavior, particularly of a hedonic nature, another study was conducted that used the same ego depletion task, scenario and dependent variables from Pretest 4. The study was a 2 (ego depletion: present/absent) X 3 (emotions: amusement/neutral/sadness) X 2 (cognitive reappraisal: low/high) and was administered to 80 undergraduate students at a southern university. First, the ego depletion manipulation that asked subjects to refrain from thinking about a white bear was administered to subjects. Next, the subjects viewed the films used in Study 3 to induce amusement and sadness. The scenario was then presented from Pretest 4 where subjects were asked to imagine that they were walking on the street and found two dollars. A snack bar was up the street and they could choose among eight items for purchase. Four of the items were more utilitarian in nature, and four were more hedonic in nature. Prices for the items were provided and ranged from $.75 to $1.25.

Manipulation Checks

Manipulation checks were performed to assess whether the films elicited the appropriate emotion from the subjects. Results revealed a main effect for amusement, $F(2, 77)=46.87$, $p<.01$ and sadness $F(2,77)=107.34$, $p<.01$. Planned contrasts showed that the amusement condition induced significantly more amusement ($M=6.57$) than the neutral and sadness conditions ($M=3.22$ and $M=2.38$, $p<.01$). Likewise, the sadness condition elicited more sadness ($M=7.44$) than the neutral and amusement conditions ($M=2.61$ and $M=1.57$, $p<.01$). The modal report for the neutral condition was 1 for all emotions.

The manipulation check for ego depletion asked subjects how worn-out and tired they felt after the task. There was no main effect for ego depletion (p>.05). For individuals in the ego depletion condition, the mean score for tiredness was 2.71, and 3.03 for those in the no-ego depletion condition. For how worn-out subjects were, means were 2.59 for individuals in the ego depletion condition and 2.95 for those in the no-ego depletion.

Findings

Results from the data indicated that individuals in the amusement condition expressed intentions to purchase a larger quantity of products (M=1.95) than individuals in the neutral and sadness conditions (M=1.16 and M=1.09, p<.05). Additionally, subjects in the amusement condition reported intentions to spend more money (M=1.82) than individuals in the neutral and sadness conditions (M=1.26 and M=1.04, p<.05).

Even though the ego depletion manipulation failed to work, according to the manipulation check, individuals in the no-ego depletion condition expressed intentions to purchase more products than individuals in the ego depletion condition (M=1.74 and M=1.07), p<.05. Also, subjects in the no-ego depletion condition reported intentions to spend more money than individuals in the ego depletion condition (M=1.67 and M=1.22), p<.10. These means were in the opposite direction than anticipated.

Results also revealed a significant three-way interaction between emotions, ego depletion and cognitive reappraisal. Low cognitive reappraisers in the sadness and no-ego depletion condition intended to spend more money and intended to purchase more hedonic products than high cognitive reappraisers in the no-ego depletion and sadness condition (M=1.21 and M=.36, p<.05).

84

CHAPTER 5

Discussion and Conclusions

INTRODUCTION

The purpose of this research has been to explore the emotion regulation consumption phenomenon by determining how, why and under what circumstances it might occur. This final chapter will include an overview and discussion of results from all studies performed. In addition, both theoretical and substantive contributions of this research will be delineated. Finally, limitations as well as directions for future research will be offered.

OVERVIEW OF RESULTS

The motivation for this research was to examine how the typical consumer might use consumption as a mechanism for managing emotions. The concept referring to this phenomenon that was used in this research is emotion regulation consumption (ERC). ERC was defined as the consumption or purchase of a good or service for the purposes of alleviating, repairing, or managing an affective state. This research was predicated on a conceptual framework using the broaden-and-build theory of positive emotions (Fredrickson 1998, 2000, 20001) along with resource-based approaches to self-regulation and mood (Aspinwall 1998, 2005; Baumeister *et al.* 1998; Tice *et al.* 2001). In addition, this research introduced a construct to the consumer research literature regarding emotion regulation known as cognitive reappraisal (Gross and John 2003).

The emotion regulation consumption phenomenon was examined using four discrete emotions (amusement, contentment, sadness and fear/anxiety). Three complete studies and a follow-up study were conducted to test hypotheses. The following sections discuss the findings from all studies conducted.

Study 1a and 1b

86

In the first between-subjects design in Study 1(a), in which the target products were the gift certificate for dinner and the gift certificate for groceries, individuals in both the amusement and sadness conditions expressed more favorable attitudes and purchase intentions for the hedonic good (gift certificate for dinner) than individuals in the neutral condition. However, significant main effects existed between the amusement and neutral conditions and the sadness and neutral conditions for purchase intentions. There were no significant differences between the positive and negative conditions.

The significant findings that existed between the sadness and neutral conditions lend support to the emotion regulation consumption phenomenon. Individuals may have indeed been attempting to down-regulate their negative emotion through the consumption of a hedonic good. However, the unexpected lack of significance between the positive and negative conditions may be attributed to affect maintenance. Research has suggested that individuals might self-regulate positive emotions in an effort to maintain positive feelings (Isen and Simmonds 1978; Pearlin and Schooler 1978; Mick and DeMoss 1990). Isen (1984, 1985, and 2000) suggested that individuals are generally motivated to maintain, even prolong, pleasant affective states. As a result, affect control processes might have manifested themselves concurrently in individuals in both the positive and negative conditions, which may be responsible for the U-shaped effect of emotions on purchase intentions for the hedonic good.

Contrary to prediction, individuals in the amusement condition were willing to pay a higher price for the hedonic good ($18.41) than individuals in the sadness condition ($16.34). Although means did not reach statistical significance, the difference of $2.07, might merit practical significance. Studies have demonstrated that individuals in whom

87

positive affect has been induced are more risk-averse (Isen *et al.* 1988). A link between affect maintenance and this aversion to risk has been observed. Distinctly, people who are feeling happy risk losing that state.

In the case of the scenario presented in Study 1, individuals were told to place a bid on an actual product and that the highest bidder would receive the product. Individuals in the amusement condition may have been willing to pay more for the hedonic product, particularly if they actually perceived that the product would prolong their current amused, playful state. Bidding a higher price would help to guard against any risk of not obtaining the product.

With regard to emotion regulation strategy, and as predicted, low cognitive reappraisers expressed more favorable attitudes, higher purchase intentions, and were willing to pay a higher price for the hedonic good (gift certificate for dinner). However, only differences between means for purchase intentions reached statistical significance. As hypothesized, low cognitive reappraisers were less able to access the internal processes necessary to down-regulate negative emotion. Consequently, this group was prone to enlisting external means, consumption being one of them, to manage their emotions.

The outcome of the second between-subjects design of Study 1(b), in which the gift certificate for music downloading and the gift certificate for an oil change was used, did not yield the results anticipated. The lack of success of this study may be due to the product choice. Even though pretests confirmed the utilitarian and hedonic nature of the products, low involvement and lack of interest for such products may explain the poor results. This outcome may also signify that consumers may view some products as more

88

effective in managing emotion than others. Subjects in this study were college students. A gift certificate for online music downloading may not have ignited the same interest as a gift certificate for dinner with friends. This may be partly due to the fact that college students are, and have been among the greatest offenders of illegal file-sharing (Timiraos 2006). Because some of them receive music for free through illicit activity, a gift certificate for music may have been of minimal value to them.

The significance differences that occurred between price, with more amused subjects willing to pay a higher price ($13.31) than sad subjects ($6.87) for the hedonic good, may also lend credence to the affect maintenance and risk-aversion proposition for individuals in a positive emotional state.

Study 2

Hypotheses 3 and 7 in Study 2 predicted that ego depletion would affect level of buying impulsiveness for a hedonic good (cheesecake). However, no significant differences were found. For levels of buying impulsiveness, subjects were asked directly to report their level of impulsivity. The lack of significant differences between the two groups may be partially due to social desirability bias, or systematic error in self-report measures that result from the desire of respondents to project more favorable images. More specifically, subjects might have provided the "correct" but dishonest response. Perhaps the use of an imaginary stimulus situation, or indirect questioning, would have been appropriate (e.g. "Sally walks into the market and sees a bakery-style cheesecake. Will she buy it?"). In such a scenario, subjects would project themselves into a situation. This indirect questioning approach may have made subjects more inclined to select the impulsive options since the "so-called buyer" would have been someone else (Fisher 1993; Rook and Fisher 1995).

Pervasive throughout the results for Study 2 was the lack of success (as predicted) of the ego depletion manipulation. In hypotheses 3 and 5, there were significant effects for ego depletion for purchase intentions; however, means were in the opposite direction anticipated. The non-ego depleted subjects expressed higher purchase intentions for the cheesecake than the ego-depleted subjects.

These unanticipated results may have been due to the ego depletion manipulation. The manipulation may have simply primed self-regulation, rather than fully depleting subjects. Ego depletion is characterized as a reduction in the self's capacity to perform subsequent tasks that require acts of self-regulation after being subjected to an initial act of self-regulation. The process of self-regulation, itself, is conceptualized as the means by which impulses are restrained and undesirable actions are replaced by more appropriate actions. Self-regulation is synonymous to a knowledge structure where self-control operates like a master schema; an initial act of self-control may prime the schema thus facilitating further self-control. In the present research, those that were in the ego depletion condition actually expressed greater regulatory behavior than those in the non-ego depletion condition, which may have been because the ego depletion task activated their regulatory schema.

Results for emotion regulation strategy were less conclusive than those in the first study. Significant differences between low and high cognitive reappraisers were found only for attitude toward the product in the fear/anxiety condition (means were in the opposite direction than predicted) and for purchase intentions in the contentment

90

condition. These inconclusive results underscore the need to examine differences in the employment of emotion regulation strategies for various, discrete emotions. Presently, emotion regulation strategies focus on broad categories of positive and negative emotions, which may obscure potentially important differences among specific emotions. For example, individuals may be able to reappraise certain emotions better than others and exhibit specific mechanisms for managing one emotion, but a different method for controlling another. Studying a broader range of negative emotions and examining the reappraisal techniques an individual employs for each would provide further insight into how such emotions are regulated.

Additionally, in Study 2, individuals were asked to report their attitudes, desire and intent to purchase a cheesecake. Even though an individual's affinity for cheesecake was assessed and included in the analysis, perhaps purchasing an entire cheesecake was too excessive. Presenting the scenario in such a way where subjects were given the option of buying a *slice* of cheesecake may have made the purchase task more amenable to subjects.

Finally, interesting findings from Study 2 provide further evidence of the emotion regulation consumption phenomenon. Individuals in the fear/anxiety condition did express higher purchase intentions for the hedonic good (cheesecake) than those in the neutral condition. Also, individuals in the contentment condition expressed higher purchase intentions for the cheesecake, which may suggest that affect maintenance was at play.

Study 3

In Study 3, an attempt was made to assess actual impulsive behavior for a hedonic good. However, results with regard to the behavioral component of the study were inconclusive. This may be partly due to the ego depletion manipulation, which was not successful. Also social desirability bias may have affected results.

The ego depletion manipulation involved subjects listing their thoughts for five minutes, but then refraining from thinking about a white bear. Every time the subjects thought about a white bear, they were to place a checkmark in a box. Those in the control condition were simply instructed to list their thoughts. The lack of success of the manipulation may have been due to low involvement of the subjects. After viewing the survey instruments that included the ego depletion task, it was noted that few subjects actually made checkmarks in the boxes. Either subjects were able to engage in exceptional mind control, or they opted not to devote a great amount of effort to the task.

Also, Study 3 was administered in groups. When subjects were presented with the purchasing situation—buying cookies or a fruit pack for a dollar—social desirability may have manifested. Individuals may have refrained from purchasing products for fear that their counterparts would view them as greedy or impulsive in nature.

Interesting results from Study 3 did reveal that individuals in the amusement condition expressed the greatest temptation to purchase product—whether it was the fruit or cookies. This finding, once again, lends support to the affect maintenance proposition.

Follow-up Study

In an effort to further examine what effect ego depletion would have on impulsive consumption of a hedonic nature, a follow-up study to Study 3 was conducted. This study yielded similar results to Study 2 with regard to the ego depletion manipulation simply priming subjects' self-regulatory sensibilities. Non-ego depleted individuals expressed higher intentions to purchase products and to spend more money than ego-depleted individuals.

Also, results regarding the effect emotions had on buying and spending intentions were similar to Study 3. Individuals in the amusement condition expressed the intent to buy and spend more money than individuals in the neutral and sadness condition. Once again, these results may suggest affect maintenance.

Finally, results did yield a significant three-way interaction between emotions, ego depletion and cognitive reappraisal. According to theoretical prediction for emotion regulation strategy, low cognitive reappraisers spent more money for the more characteristically hedonic products than high cognitive reappraisers—demonstrating the propensity of low reappraisers to use external mechanisms (consumption) to down-regulate sadness.

CONTRIBUTIONS

Several theoretical and substantive contributions are offered from the findings of this research. Theoretically, this research provides further understanding as to why and how people attempt to manage their emotions, particularly negative ones. The broaden-and-build theory explains that positive emotions undo the effects of negative emotions (Fredrickson 1998, 2000). Consuming hedonic products—products from which consumers derive some feelings of enjoyment—can help to mitigate negative emotions. Additionally, ego depleted individuals may be more prone to consuming, or purchasing, products on impulse. However, consuming products to manage emotions might also be affected by internal processes related to an individual's ability to regulate emotion. Cognitive reappraisal, one emotion regulation strategy that manifests itself as a trait, or individual difference, may affect consumption behavior as well.

Studying ERC can lead to greater enlightenment regarding the effect that pre-existing emotions have on consumption behavior. This can guide marketers in developing marketing communications as well as planning the retail environment. Additionally, understanding more about ERC and impulse-control can help explain why individuals engage in aversive consumption, such as overeating and excessive drinking. These findings could potentially have strong implications for consumer welfare. The following section enumerates these and other contributions of this research.

Theoretical Contributions

This research helped to provide some insight into why and how people might engage in consumption activities to regulate or manage emotions in everyday life. The broaden-and-build theory proposes that positive emotions undo the effects of negative emotions. Evidence from this research demonstrates how people might consume products of a hedonic nature to "down-regulate" negative emotions such as sadness, thereby infusing positive emotions into their lives. Further, results also indicate that people may manage positive emotions, such as amusement and contentment, by engaging in consumption to maintain their emotional state. This supports the affect maintenance proposition.

Emotion regulation consumption may be contingent on an individual's available supply of psychological resources. When an individual's resources have been depleted, exercising self-control may become very difficult (Baumeister *et al.*1998). Several of the ego depletion manipulations administered in this research, particularly the pretests, were successful at depleting the ego. These individuals with depleted egos were more likely to engage in impulsive hedonic consumption. Research suggests that hedonic products can be therapeutic and activate feelings of enjoyment. Positive feelings and emotions obtained from these hedonic products can help to restore the depleted ego (Tice *et al.* 2007). Hence, emotion regulation consumption, even of an impulsive nature, may also be more likely to occur in individuals whose psychological resources have been depleted.

This research also provides some preliminary evidence that regulatory resources operate like a knowledge structure and the priming of self-regulation can occur. Activation of self-regulation could then enable individuals to exercise impulse-control.

Individual differences in the way individuals cognitively exercise control over their emotions may also have some impact on consumption behavior. Cognitive reappraisal, one common emotion regulation strategy, involves construing a potentially emotion-eliciting situation in a way that changes its emotional impact. This research suggests that individuals less able to exercise internal control of their negative emotions (particularly sadness) may be more likely to use hedonic consumption as a way to manage their emotions. At the same time, exploring emotion regulation strategy with regard to specific emotions also merits attention. Individuals may cognitive reappraise different emotions with varying degrees of facility.

This research also explored emotion regulation consumption by focusing on the study of discrete emotions. Much of the consumer research literature has characterized affective states along two dimensions—good versus bad or positive versus negative. However, different emotions (ie. fear, sadness, amusement, contentment) result in different appraisals of one's environment (Lazarus 1984, 1994; Smith and Ellsworth

95

1985) and invoke various action tendencies. These specific emotions also affect

judgment and choice differently (Lerner and Keltner 2000; Raghunathan and Corfin

2004). For example, in this research, even emotions of the same valence (sadness versus

fear/anxiety) yielded different behavioral outcomes, particularly with regard to emotion

regulation strategy.

Substantive Contributions

Research from studies on emotion regulation consumption and self-regulatory

processes may have special implications for marketing. For example, consumers pre-

existing emotions and available supply of psychological resources can affect their

shopping behavior. Understanding dynamics such as these can help retailers in shaping

the retail environment, or merchandising. For example, those individuals whose egos

have been depleted may engage in more impulsive purchasing behavior. Research shows

that as much as 85% of purchasing decisions are made at the point of purchase (Casey

2002). Therefore, marketers might continue to strategically consider the placement of

characteristically hedonic products in the store environment. Empirical evidence from

this research might suggest that placing hedonic products near the front of the store

(particularly supermarkets) can be an effective way to appeal to hedonic impulses and

subsequently increase customer purchases.

Further, understanding consumer emotions and interpersonal processes can help

in planning and integrating effective sales person responses to consumers (Menon and

Dube 2000; Mick, DeMoss and Faber 1992). Customers expect service providers to

respond to their emotions, whether positive or negative, in a supportive manner. The ability of a service provider to do so may impact the service sequence thus leading to varying levels of satisfaction (Menon and Dube 2004).

Employing insight gleaned from the emotion regulation consumption phenomenon can assist marketers in designing and developing effective marketing communications for hedonic products. Specifically, this research helped to demonstrate that individuals who are experiencing an emotion such as sadness may be more likely to engage in hedonic consumption to down-regulate negative emotions, whereas an individual experiencing positive emotion such as amusement may be more likely to purchase a hedonic product in order to maintain or even up-regulate positive emotion. Managers might acknowledge the gamut of emotions experienced by consumers and make efforts to remind consumers of the feeling that using their product might generate, which may indeed help consumers to attain a desired feeling.

Understanding emotion regulation consumption and impulse-control can also provide more insight into why individuals engage in aversive consumption, such as overeating, excessive drinking and promiscuous sexual behavior. Regulating emotional distress often takes precedence over impulse-control and individuals may be engaging in these consumption activities to achieve short-term gratification from negative feelings. For example, emotional eating is a common phenomenon in response to stress or sadness (D'Arrigo 2007). Research has shown that emotional eating is related to reliance on emotion-oriented coping and avoidance distraction in both eating-disordered women and relatively healthy women (Spoor 2007). Educating and making individuals aware of why they might be engaging in such destructive behavioral patterns and, thus, encouraging more healthy alternatives as a way of managing emotions might be an initial step towards behavior change.

LIMITATIONS

Due to forced exposure to stimuli, the experimental settings in this research restrict the generalizability of results. However, such limitations are consistent with most experimental studies. Duplicating a real-word ERC scenario has its implementation challenges in a laboratory setting. For example, emotions induced in an experimental study may prove to be more ephemeral than those experienced in real-world situations. Also manipulation checks established that the films used to induce the emotions in this research were effective; nevertheless, the use of films does require an aesthetic emotion (Frijda 1989) where subjects must be willing to enlist their imaginations and suspend disbelief. Films are illusions of reality and not actual, real-life situations.

The results of the ego depletion manipulations in this research were weak—with some manipulations placing individuals in more self-regulatory states. Implementing other procedures that place demands on attentional, emotional or mental self-control, or even more manipulations truer to life, might yield different results.

Additionally, the low involvement of subjects may have also played a role in the inefficacy of some of the ego depletion manipulations in this research. Some of this low involvement may have been due to the administration of the experiments in classroom settings. Conducting the studies in classrooms may have also attributed to social desirability bias, particularly in the third study where individuals were given the option of purchasing products. Subjects may have been reticent about making such purchases in the presence of peers.

Social desirability may have also played a role with regard to the scenario and measure in the second study that was used to assess level of buying impulsiveness. Using indirect questioning may have been a more effective way to ascertain subjects' impulsivity propensity.

Finally, the products used in this research may have constrained subjects with regard to their emotion regulation management. Subsequently, products purchased or consumed by individuals to regulate their emotions may be very unique to that individual and varied.

FUTURE RESEARCH

A wealth of research opportunities exist for the exploration of emotion regulation consumption. This research examined four commonly experienced discrete emotions. More emotions experienced in the consumption process might also be studied (e.g. guilt, anger). Additionally, one emotion regulation strategy, cognitive reappraisal, was examined in this research. Cognitive reappraisal is an antecedent-focused emotion regulation strategy—it occurs early and intervenes before emotion response tendencies have been fully activated. Response-focused emotion regulation strategies, such as expressive suppression, might also be examined within the context of ERC (Gross and John 2003). These strategies usually come later in the emotion-generative process and modify the behavioral aspect of emotion response tendencies. The implications of such an emotion regulation strategy might have differential effects on ERC.

Also, future research might explore the link between emotional intelligence and emotion regulation consumption. Emotional intelligence is related to an individual's ability to perceive, facilitate, understand and manage emotions (Mayer and Salovey

1997). Researchers have begun to examine emotional intelligence within the framework of consumption (Kidwell, Hardesty and Childers 2008). For example, an individual's ability to identify and use relevant emotions may impact their consumption behavior.

This research focused primarily on material or tangible products (with the exception of Study1). Further research might explore ERC using both material and experiential products. Research by Von Boven and Gilovich (2003) suggests that individuals feel that experiential products place them in happier mood states than material products. A study of material versus experiential products in the context of ERC could yield illuminating results.

Furthermore, in this research, positive emotions were juxtaposed against negative emotions and one of the primary focuses of this investigation was in ascertaining differences between discrete emotions of opposing valences. Future research might examine the effect that arousal and emotional intensity have on the ERC phenomenon.

As mentioned earlier, a rich body of consumer welfare research might also emerge from further examination of the ERC phenomenon. With health issues related to obesity plaguing society, investigating the connection between emotions and aversive health-affecting behavior, such as overeating, might be a nascent understanding of such destructive behavior.

A body of literature has emerged on the emotional consequences and tradeoffs of indulgences and hedonic consumption (Luce, Bettman and Payne 2001; Ramanathan and Williams 2007; Chitturi, Raghunathan and Mahajan 2007). Studies could be conducted that extend the ERC phenomenon within these contexts. More specifically, after consuming or purchasing a product to manage an emotion, what subsequent emotions might individuals feel?

The primary theoretical basis for this research was the broaden-and-build theory of positive emotions. The broaden-and-build theory helps to explain the adaptive quality of positive emotions. According to the theory, positive emotions expand cognition and behavioral tendencies. Future research might examine the effect that various discrete positive emotions have on decision-making ability within a consumption context. For example, might an emotion such as pride have the same broadening effect as an emotion like contentment?

The results regarding the relationship between emotions and the price individuals were willing to pay for a hedonic product were somewhat enlightening, although in the opposite direction than what was predicted. Individuals in the positive emotion condition (amusement) exhibited less price sensitive behavior. More research might explore the affect that pre-exiting emotions have on consumer responses to price.

Marketers have long recognized the role that emotions play in advertising (Edell and Burke 1987; Holbrook and Batra 1986). Future research might explore consumers' reactions to advertisements containing "ERC language" (e.g., "Have a Coke and a smile," "The Joy of Cola—Pepsi , "The best part of waking up is Folgers in your cup"). This might provide some additional direction and understanding regarding promoting products of a hedonic nature.

Finally, deeper and richer insight about the ERC phenomenon might also be gleaned by revisiting the work of Mick and DeMoss (1990) and applying a qualitative approach to exploring the personal efforts of individuals that have used consumption or buying as a way to manage emotions. Studying ERC in an experimental context definitely has its merits, but a qualitative approach might provide additional insight as to what type of consumption different people use to manage emotions and what additional emotions are key in the ERC phenomenon.

CONCLUDING REMARKS

This research has taken a look at how individuals might use consumption as a way to manage their emotions. Additionally, the effects of regulatory depletion were examined to see how a deficiency in these resources might affect hedonic consumption, particularly of an impulsive nature. This research offers an initial investigation into the role that pre-existing emotions and self-regulation play in the consumption process. In addition to the cognitive processes that have been extensively studied in the consumer research literature, more attention should be accorded to the study of emotions and impulse-control which greatly affect consumption.

REFERENCES

American Psychiatric Association (2000), *Diagnostic and Statistical Manual of Mental Disorders:* DSM-IV-TR, Vol. 4, Washington, DC: American Psychiatric Association.

Abrahams, Ben (1997), "It's all in the Mind," *Marketing,* 31-33.

Andrade, Eduardo B. (2005), "Behavioral Consequences of Affect: Combining Evaluative and Regulatory Mechanisms," *Journal of Consumer Research,* 32 (12), 355-362.

Aspinwall, Lisa G. (1998), "Rethinking the Role of Positive Affect in Self-Regulation," *Motivation and Emotion, (*22), 1-32.

----- (2005), "The Psychology of Future-Oriented Thinking: From Achievement to Proactive Coping, Adaptation, and Aging," *Motivation and Emotion,* 29, 203-235.

Babin, Barry J., William R. Darden, and Mitch Griffin (1994), "Work and/or Fun: Measuring Hedonic and Utilitarian Shopping," *Journal of Consumer Research,* 20 (March), 644-656.

-----, James S. Boles, and William R. Darden (1995), "Salesperson Stereotypes, Consumer Emotions, and their Impact on Information Processing," *Academy of Marketing Science Journal,* 23 (Spring), 94.

-----, William R. Darden (1995), "Consumer Self-Regulation in a Retail Environment," *Journal of Retailing,* 71 (Spring), 47-70.

----- (1996), "Good and Bad Shopping Vibes: Spending and Patronage Satisfaction," *Journal of Business Research,* 35 (March), 201-206.

Bagozzi, Richard P., Mahesh Gopinath, and Prashanth U. Nyer (1999), "The Role of Emotions in Marketing," *Academy of Marketing Science Journal,* 27 (Spring), 184.

-----, David J. Moore (1994), "Public Service Advertisements: Emotions and Empathy Guide Prosocial Behavior," *Journal of Marketing,* 58 (1), 56-70.

Batra, Rajeev and Olli T. Ahtola (1991), "Measuring the Hedonic and Utilitarian Sources of Consumer Attitudes," *Marketing Letters,* 2 (4), 159-170.

Baumeister, Roy F. (2002), "Ego Depletion and Self-Control Failure: An Energy Model of the Self's Executive Function," *Self & Identity,* 1 (4), 129-136.

---- (2002), "Yielding to Temptation: Self-Control Failure, Impulsive Purchasing, and Consumer Behavior," *Journal of Consumer Research,* 28, (3) 670-676.

-----, E. Bratslavsky, Mark Muraven and Dianne M. Tice(1998), "Ego Depletion: Is the Active Self a Limited Resource?" *Journal of Personality & Social Psychology,* 74 (5), 1252-1265.

-----, Mark Muraven (2000), "Ego Depletion: A Resource Model of Volition, Self-Regulation, and Controlled Processing," *Social Cognition,* 18, 130.

Bazerman, Max H., Ann E. Tenbrunsel, and Kimberly Wade-Benzoni (1998), "Negotiating with Yourself and Losing: Making Decisions with Competing Internal Preferences," *Academy of Management the Academy of Management Review,* 23 (April), 225.

Beatty, Sharon E. and M. E. Ferrell (1998), "Impulse Buying: Modeling its Precursors," *Journal of Retailing,* 74 (Summer), 169.

Bernthal, Matthew J., David Crockett, Randell Rose (2005), "Credit Cards as Lifestyle Facilitators," *Journal of Consumer Research,* 32 (6), 130-45.

Bitner, Mary J. (1992), "Servicescapes: The Impact of Physical Surroundings on Customers and Employees," *Journal of Marketing,* 56 (April), 57

Bohner, Gerd and Norbert Schwarz (1993), "Mood States Influence the Production of Persuasive Arguments," *Communication Research,* 20 (October), 696.

Burke, Marian C. and Julie A. Edell (1989), "The Impact of Feelings on Ad-Based Affect and Cognition," *Journal of Marketing Research,* 26 (2), 69-83.

Carnevale, Peter J. D. and Alice M. Isen (1986), "The Influence of Positive Affect and Visual Access on the Discovery of Integrative Solutions, "*Organizational Behavior & Human Decision Processes,* 37 (2), 1.

Casey, John (2002), "Planned' Impulse Purchases: Grocery Store Head Game," MedicineNet.com.

Chitturi, Ravindra, Rajagopal Raghunathan, and Vihay Mahajan (2007), "Form Versus Function: How the Intensities of Sepcific Emotions Evoked in Functuional Versus Hedonic Trade-Offs Mediate Product Preferences," *Journal of Marketing Research,* (November), 702-714.

Cialdini, Robert J., B. Darby and J. Vincent (1973), " Transgression and Altruism: A Case Hedonism," *Journal of Experimental Social Psychology,* 9, 502-556.

Clark, Margaret S. and Alice M. Isen (1982), "Towards Understanding the Relationship between Feeling States and Social Behavior." in *Cognitive Social Psychology,* Hastorf, H.A. and Alice M. Isen, ed. New York: Elsevier/North-Holland, 73-108.

Cohen, Joel B. and Eduardo B. Andrade (2004), "Affective Intuition and Task-Contingent Affect Regulation," *Journal of Consumer Research,* 31 (9), 358-367.

Csikszentmihalyi, Mihaly (1990), *Flow: The Psychology of Optimal Experience.* New York: Harper and Row.

D'Arrigo, Terri (2007), "Emotional Eating: A Sneak Attack on Weight Loss," *Diabetes Forecast*, July, 23.

Dawson, Scott, Peter H. Bloch, and Nancy M. Ridgway (1990), "Shopping Motives, Emotional States, and Retail Outcomes," *Journal of Retailing,* 66 (Winter), 408-427.

Derbaix, Christian M. (1995), "The Impact of Affective Reactions on Attitudes Toward the Advertisement and the Brand: A Step Toward Ecological Validity," *Journal of Marketing Research,* 32 (November), 470-479.

Derryberry, Douglas and Don M. Tucker (1992), "Neural Mechanisms of Emotion," *Journal of Consulting and Clinical Psychology,* 60 (June), 329-338.

Dhar, Ravi and Klaus Wertenbroch (2000), "Consumer Choice between Hedonic and Utilitarian Goods," Journal *of Marketing Research,* 37 (Feb), 60-71.

Dholakia, Utpal M., Mahesh Gopinath and Richard P. Bagozzi (2005), "The Role of Desires in Sequential Impulsive Choice," *Organizational Behavior and Human Decision Processes*, 98, 179-194.

Eckman, Paul, W. V. Friesen and Sonya Ancoli (1980), "Facial Signs of Emotional Experience," *Journal of Personality & Social Psychology,* 39, 1124-1134.

Edell, Julie A. and Marian C. Burke (1987), "The Power of Feelings in Understanding Advertising Effects," *Journal of Consumer Research*, 14 (December): 421-33.

Elliott, Richard (1994), "Addictive Consumption: Function and Fragmentation in Postmodernity," *Journal of Consumer Policy,* 17 (June), 159-179.

Epstein, Seymour (1972), "The Nature of Anxiety with Emphasis upon its Relationship to Expectancy," in *Anxiety: Current Trends in Theory and Research,* C.D. Spielberger, ed. New York, NY: Academic Press, 292-338.

Faber, Ronald J. and Gary A. Christenson (1996), "In the Mood to Buy: Differences in the Mood States Experienced by Compulsive Buyers and Other Consumers," *Psychology & Marketing,* 13 (12), 803-819.

Fisher, Robert F. (1993), "Social Desirability Bias and the Validity of Indirect Questioning," *Journal of Consumer Research,* 20, 303-313.

Folkman, S. and R.S. Lazarus (1984), *Stress, Appraisal and Coping,* New York: Springer.

Franko, D. L., T .A. Powers, D.C. Zuroff, D. S. Moskowitz (1985), "Children and Affect: Strategies for Self-Regulation and Sex Differences in Sadness," *American Journal of Orthopsychiatry,* 55, 210-219.

Frederickson, Barbara L., Robert W. Levenson (1998), "Positive Emotions Speed Recovery from the Cardiovascular Sequelae of Negative Emotions," *Cognition & Emotion,* 12 (3), 191-220.

-----, Roberto A. Mancuso, Christine Branigan and Michael Tugade (2000), "The Undoing Effect of Positive Emotions," *Motivation & Emotion,* 24 (12), 237-258.

----- (2001), "The Role of Positive Emotions in Positive Psychology," *American Psychologist,* 56 (3), 218-226.

---- (2002), "Positive Emotions Trigger Upward Spirals Toward Emotional Well-being," *Psychological Science,* 13 (March), 172-175.

---- (2003), "The Value of Positive Emotions," *American Scientist,* 91 (7), 330-335.

-----, Michael M. Tugade, Christian E. Waugh and Gregory R. Larkin (2003), "What Good are Positive Emotions in Crises? A Prospective Study of Resilience and Emotions Following the Terrorist Attacks on the United States on September 11th, 2001," *Journal of Personality & Social Psychology,* 84 (2), 365-376.

-----, Christine Branigan (2005), "Positive Emotions Broaden the Scope of Attention and Thought-action Repertoires," *Cognition & Emotion,* 19 (4), 313-332.

Frijda, Nico (1986), *The Emotions: Studies in Emotion and Social Interaction*, New York: Cambridge University Press.

----- (1989), "Aesthetic Emotion and Reality," *American Psychologist,* 44, 1546-1547.

Fry, C. L. (1975), "Tactual Illusions," *Perception and Motor Skill,* 40, 955-60.

Gardner, Meryl P. (1985), "Mood States and Consumer Behavior: A Critical Review," *Journal of Consumer Research,* 12 (December), 281-300.

-----, Dennis W. Rook (1988), "Effects of Impulse Purchases on Consumers' Affective States," *Advances in Consumer Research,* 15, 127-130.

-----, Ronald P. Hill (1988), "Consumers' Mood States: Antecedents and Consequences of Experiential Versus Informational Strategies for Brand Choice," *Psychology & Marketing,* 5 (Summer), 169-182.

-----, John Scott (1990), "Product Type: A Neglected Moderator of the Effects of Mood," *Advances in Consumer Research,* 17, 585-589.

Garg, Nitika, Brian Wansink, and J. J. Inman (2007), "The Influence of Incidental Affect on Consumers' Food Intake," *Journal of Marketing,* 71 (1), 194-206.

----- (1998), "Antecedent- and Response-Focused Emotion Regulation: Divergent Consequences for Experience, Expression and Physiology," *Journal of Personality and Social Psychology,* 74 (January), 224-237.

-----, Oliver P. John (2003), "Individual Differences in Two Emotion Regulation Processes: Implications for Affect, Relationships, and Well-being," *Journal of Personality & Social Psychology,* 85 (8), 348-362.

-----, Jane M. Richards, and O.P. John (2006), "Emotion Regulation in Everyday," in *Life Emotion Regulation in Families,* D.K. Snyder, J.A. Simpson, and J.N. Hughes, ed. Washington, D.C.: American Psychological Association, 1-34.

Hirschman, Elizabeth, C., Morris B. Holbrook (1982), "Hedonic Consumption: Emerging Concepts, Methods and Propositions," *Journal of Marketing,* 46 (Summer), 92-101.

----- (1992), "The Consciousness of Addiction: Toward a General Theory of Compulsive Consumption," *Journal of Consumer Research,* 19 (Sep), 155-179.

Hoch, Stephen J. and George F. Loewenstein (1991), "Time-Inconsistent Preferences and Consumer Self-Control," *Journal of Consumer Research,* 17 (Mar), 492-507..

Holbrook, Morris B. and Elizabeth C. Hirschman (1982), "The Experiential Aspects of Consumption: Consumer Fantasies, Feelings, and Fun," *Journal of Consumer Research,* 9 (Sept), 132-140.

----- and Rajeev Batra (1986), "Assessing the Role of Emotions as Mediators of Consumer Responses to Advertising" *Journal of Consumer Research*, 14 (December): 404-20

Isen, Alice M., and S.F. Simmonds (1978), "The Effect of Feeling Good on a Helping Task that is Incompatible with Good Mood " *Journal of Personality and Social Psychology,* 36, 1-12.

-----, Robert Patrick (1983), "The Effect of Positive Feelings on Risk Taking: When the Chips are Down," *Organizational Behavior and Human Performance,* 31 (April), 194-202.

-----, K. A Daubman (1984), " the Influence of Affect on Categorization," *Journal of Personality and Social Psychology,* 47, 1206-1217.

------ (1984), "The Influence of Positive Affect on Decision Making and Cognitive Organization," *Advances in Consumer Research,* 11, 534-537.

-----, Kimberly A. Daubman, and Gary P. Nowicki (1987), "Positive Affect Facilitates Creative Problem Solving," *Journal of Personality and Social Psychology,* 52 (June), 1206-1217.

-----, Nehemia Geva (1987), "The Influence of Positive Affect on Acceptable Level of Risk: The Person with a Large Canoe has a Large Worry," *Organizational Behavior and Human Decision Processes,* 39 (April), 145-154.

-----, M. M. S. Johnson, E. Mertz, and G.F. Robinson (1985), "The Influence of Positive Affect on the Unusualness of Word Associations," *Journal of Personality and Social Psychology,* 48, 1413-1426.

----- (2000), "Positive Affect" in Lewis, M. and J. M. Haviland-Jones, ed. *Handbook of Emotions,* New York: Guilford Press, 417-435.

Izard, Carroll (1977), *Human Emotions.* New York: Plenum.

-----, B.P. Ackerman (2000), "Motivational, Organizational, and Regulatory and Functions of Discrete Emotions," in *Handbook of Emotions,* Lewis M. L. and J.M. Haviland-Jones, ed. New York: Guliford Press, 523-564.

Kacen, Jacqueline J. (1994), "Phenomenological Insights in Mood and Mood-Related Consumer Behaviors," *Advances in Consumer Research,* 21, 519-525.

---- (1998), "A Conceptual Overview of Consumers' Mood Management Strategies," *American Marketing Association Conference Proceedings,* 9, 140.

-----, Julie A. Lee (2002), "The Influence of Culture on Consumer Impulsive Buying Behavior," *Journal of Consumer Psychology,* 12, 163-176.

Kahn, Barbara E. and Alice M. Isen (1993), "The Influence of Positive Affect on Variety Seeking among Safe, Enjoyable Products," *Journal of Consumer Research,* 20 (September), 257-270.

Kelley, S. W., and K. Hoffman (1997), "An Investigation of Positive Affect, Prosocial Behaviors and Service Quality," *Journal of Retailing,* 73, 407-427.

Kidwell, Blair, David M. Hardesty and Terry L. Childers (2008). "Consumer Emotional Intelligence: Conceptualization, Measurement, and the Prediction of Consumer Decision Making," *Journal of Consumer Research*, 35.

Kimchi, R. (1992), "Primacy of Wholistic Processing and Global/Local Paradigm: A Critical Review," *Psychological Bulletin*, 112, 24-38.

Knowles, Patricia A., Stephen J. Grove, and Gregory M. Pickett (1993), "Mood and the Service Customer: Review and Propositions," *The Journal of Services Marketing*, 7, 41-52.

Larsen, Randy J. (2000), "Toward a Science of Mood Regulation," *Psychological Inquiry*, 11, 129-141.

Lazarus, R. S. and E. Alfert (1964), "Short-Circuiting of Threat by Experimentally Altering Cognitive Appraisal," *Journal of Abnormal and Social Psychology*, 69, 195-205.

Lazarus, Richard S. (1991), "Cognition and Motivation in Emotion," *American Psychologist*, 46 (4), 352-367.

---- (1991), "Progress on a Cognitive-Motivational-Relational Theory of Emotion," *The American Psychologist*, 46 (August), 819-834.

Lerner, Jennifer S. and Dacher Keltner (2000), "Beyond Valence: Toward a Model of Emotion-Specific Influences on Judgment and Choice," *Cognition & Emotion*, 14 (7), 473-493.

Loewenstein, George (1996), "Out of Control: Visceral Influences on Behavior," *Organizational Behavior and Human Decision Processes*, 65, 272-292.

Louro, Maria J., Rik Pieters, and Marcel Zeelenberg (2005), "Negative Returns on Positive Emotions: The Influence of Pride and Self-Regulatory Goals on Repurchase Decisions," *Journal of Consumer Research*, 31 (March), 833-840.

Luce, Mary F., James R. Bettman, and John W. Payne (2001), "An Integrated Model of Trade-Off Difficulty and Consumer Choice," *Journal of Consumer Research*, 11-35.

Luo, Xueming (2005), "How does Shopping with Others Influence Impulsive Purchasing?" *Journal of Consumer Psychology*, 15, 288-294.

Mano, Haim (1999), "The Influence of Pre-Existing Negative Affect on Store Purchase Intentions," *Journal of Retailing*, 75 (Summer), 149-172.

----- (1999), "The Influence of Pre-Existing Negative Effect on Store Purchase Intentions," *Journal of Retailing,* 75, 149-183.

Manucia, G., D. Baumann, R. Cialdini (1984), "Mood Influences on Helping: Direct Effects or Side Effects?" *Journal of Personality and Social Psychology,* 46, 357-64.

Mayer, John D., and Peter Salovey, P. (1997), "What is Emotional Intelligence?" In P. Salovey and D. Sluyter (Eds.), *Emotional Development and Emotional Intelligence: Implications for Educators.* New York: Basic Books, 3-33.

Mayne, Tracy J. (2001), "Emotions and Health," in *Emotions: Current Issues and Future Directions,* Mayne, Tracy J. and George A. Bonanno, ed. New York: Guilford Press.

Meadowcraft, J.M., and D. Zillmann (1987), "Women's Comedy Preferences during the Menstrual Cycle," *Communication Research,* 14, 204-218.

Menon, Kalyani and Laurette Dube (2000), "Ensuring Greater Satisfaction by Engineering Salesperson Response to Customer Emotions," *Journal of Retailing,* 76, 285-307.

Mick, David G. and Michelle Demoss (1990), "Self-Gifts: Phenomenological Insights from Four Contexts," *Journal of Consumer Research,* 17 (12), 322-332.

-----, Michelle Demoss, and Ronald J. Faber (1992), "A Projective Study of Motivations and Meanings of Self-Gifts: Implications for Retail Management," *Journal of Retailing,* 68, 122-144.

Mittal, Banwari (1995), "A Comparative Analysis of Four Scales of Consumer Involvement," *Psychology & Marketing,* 12 (October), 663-682.

Moore, David J., William D. Harris, and Hong C. Chen (1995), "Affect Intensity: An Individual Difference Response to Advertising Appeals," *Journal of Consumer Research,* 22 (9), 154-164.

Morris, W.N. and N.P. Reilly (1987), "Toward the Self-Regulation of Mood: Theory and Research," *Motivation and Emotion,* 11, 215-249.

Ochsner, K. and James J. Gross (2005), "The Cognitive Control of Emotion," *Trends in Cognitive Sciences,* 9, 242-249.

O'Guinn, Thomas C. and Ronald J. Faber (1989), "Compulsive Buying: A Phenomenological Exploration," *Journal of Consumer Research,* 16 (9), 147157.

Okada, Erica M. (2005), "Justification Effects on Consumer Choice of Hedonic and Utilitarian Goods," Journal *of Marketing Research,* 42 (February), 43-54.

Pearlin, Leonard I. and Carmi Schooler (1978), "The Structure of Coping," *Journal of Health & Social Behavior,* 19 (3), 2-21.

Pechmann, Cornelia *et al.* (2005), "Impulsive and Self-Conscious: Adolescents' Vulnerability to Advertising and Promotion," *Journal of Public Policy & Marketing,* 24, 202-221.

Pellegrini, A. D. (1987), *Applied Child Study: A Developmental Approach .* Hillsdale, New Jersey: Lawrence Erlbaum Associates, Publishers.

Perry, Ann (2002), "Excessive Spending, Debt seen as Abusive," *The San Diego Union-Tribune,* Business H-1.

Pham, Michel T. (1998), "Representatives, Relevance, and the use of Feelings in Decision Making," *Journal of Consumer Research,* 25 (9), 144-159.

-----, Joel B. Cohen, John Q. Pracejus and G. David Huges. (2001), "Affect Monitoring and the Primacy of Feelings in Judgment," *Journal of Consumer Research,* 28 (September), 167-188.

Plutchik, Robert (1980), *Emotions, A a Psychoevolutionary Synthesis.* New York: Harper and Row.

Posner, M.I. and C.R.R. Snyder (1975), "Attention and Cognitive Control " in *Information Processing and Cognition: The Loyola Symposium,* R.L. Solso, ed. Hillsdale, NJ: Lawrence Erlbaum Associates Inc.

Puri, Radhika (1996), " Measuring and Modifying Consumer Impulsiveness: A Cost-Accessibility Framework," *Journal of Consumer Psychology,* 5, 87-113.

-----, Michel T. Pham (1999), "All Negative Moods are Not Equal: Motivational Influences of Anxiety and Sadness on Decision Making," *Organizational Behavior & Human Decision Processes,* 79 (7), 56-77.

Raghunathan, Rajagopal and Yaacov Trope (2002), "Walking the Tightrope between Feeling Good and being Accurate: Mood-as-a-Resource in Processing Persuasive Messages," *Journal of Personality and Social Psychology,* 83 (September), 510-525.

-----, Kim P. Corfman (2004), "Sadness as Pleasure-Seeking Prime and Anxiety as Attentiveness Prime: The "Different Affect–Different Effect" (DADE) Model," *Motivation & Emotion,* 28 (3), 23-47.

-----, Michel T. Pham, and Kim P. Corfman (2006), "Informational Properties of Anxiety and Sadness, and Displaced Coping," *Journal of Consumer Research,* 32 (3), 596-601.

Ramanthan, Suresh and Patti Williams(2007), "Immediate and Delayed Emotional Consequences of Indulgence: The Moderatin Influece of Personality Type on Mixed Emotions," Journal of Consumer Research, 34, 212-224.

Richards, Jane M. and James J. Gross (2000), "Emotion Regulation and Memory: The Cognitive Costs of Keeping One's Cool," *Journal of Personality & Social Psychology,* 79 (9), 410-424.

Richins, Marsha L. (1997), "Measuring Emotions in the Consumption Experience," *Journal of Consumer Research,* 24 (September), 127-146.

Rook, Dennis W. (1987), "The Buying Impulse," *Journal of Consumer Research,* 14 (9), 189-199.

---- (1995), "Normative Influences on Impulsive Buying Behavior," *Journal of Consumer Research,* 22 (December), 305-313.

Rubin, Rita (2006), "1 in 5 Adults have a Close Relative Who is Or was Addicted to Drugs or Alcohol ; in Tim Ryan's Family, He is the Addict," *USA TODAY,* (July 20), A.1.

Scheier, M. F.and C.S. Carver (1987), "Dispositional Optimism and Physical Well-being: The Influence of Generalized Expectancies on Health," *Journal of Personality,* 55, 169-210.

Schwarz, Norbet and G.L. Clore (1983), "Mood, Misattribution, and Judgements of Well-being: Informative and Directive Functions of Affective States," *Journal of Personality and Social Psychology,* 45, 513-523.

Seaman, G. and J.G. Schwarz (1974), "Success and Failure and Preference for Immediate Versus Delayed Reward." *Journal of Research in Personality,* 384-394.

Sfiligoj, Eric (1996), "Helping the 'Little Guy' to Merchandise," *Beverage World,* 115 (June 30), 20.

Sherman, Elaine, Anil Mathur, and Ruth B. Smith (1997), "Store Environment and Consumer Purchase Behavior: Mediating Role of Consumer Emotions," *Psychology & Marketing (1986-1998),* 14 (July), 361-378.

Smith, C.A. and C.P. Ellsworth (1985), "Patterns of Cognitive Appraisal in Emotion," *Journal of Personality and Social Psychology,* 48, 813-38.

Smith, Don (1996), "The Joy of Candy," *National Petroleum News.*

Spoor, S.T. (2007), "New Life Sciences Study Results from University of Texas, Department of Psychology," Women's Health Weekly, June 28, 149.

Stafford, Marla R. and Ellen Day (1995), "Retail Services Advertising: The Effects of Appeal, Medium," *Journal of Advertising,* 24 (Spring), 57-71.

Taylor, Charles R., Gordon E. Miracle, and R. D. Wilson (1997), "The Impact of Information Level on the Effectiveness of U.S. and Korean Television Commercials," *Journal of Advertising,* 26 (Spring), 1-18.

Taylor, Shelley E. and Marci Lobel (1989), "Social Comparison Activity Under Threat: Downward Evaluation and Upward Contacts," *Psychological Review,* 96 (October), 569-575.

Termine N. T. and C.E. Izard (1988), "Infants' Responses to their Mothers' Expressions of Joy and Sadness," *Developmental Psychology,* 24, 223-229.

Thayer, Robert E. (1996), *The Origin of Everyday Moods.* New York: Oxford University Press.

Timiraos, Nick (2006), "Free Legal and Ignored; Colleges Offer Music Downloads, But Their Students Just Say No; Too Many Strings Attached," *Wall Street Journal,* July 6, B1.

Tice, Dianne M., Ellen Bratslavsky, and Roy F. Baumeister (2001), "Emotional Distress Regulation Takes Precedence Over Impulse Control: If You Feel Bad, Do It!" *Journal of Personality & Social Psychology,* 80 (1), 53-67.

Tice, Dianne M, Roy F. Baumeister, Dikla Shmueli and Mark Muraven (2007), "Restoring the Sefl: Postive Affect Helps Improve Self-Regulation Following Ego Depletion," *Journal of Experimental Social Psychology*, March, 379-384.

Tomkins, Silvan (1962; 1963;), *Affect/Imagery/Consciousness.* New York: Springer.

Totterdell, Peter *et al.* (1996), "Fingerprinting Time Series: Dynamic Patterns in Self-Report and Performance Measures Uncovered by a Graphical Non-Linear Method," *The British Journal of Psychology,* 87 (February), 43-60.

Trope, Yaacov and Efrat Neter (1994), "Reconciling Competing Motives in Self-Evaluation: The Role of Self-Control in Feedback Seeking," *Journal of Personality & Social Psychology,* 66 (4), 646-657.

----- (1994), "Reconciling Competing Motives in Self-Evaluation: The Role of Self-Control in Feedback Seeking," *Journal of Personality and Social Psychology,* 66 (April), 646-657.

Tugade, Michele M. and Barbara L. Fredrickson (2004), "Resilient Individuals use Positive Emotions to Bounce Back from Negative Emotional Experiences," *Journal of Personality & Social Psychology,* 86 (2), 320-333.

Underwood, B., D.L. Rosenhan, B.S. Moore (1973), "Affect Moderates Self-Gratification," *Developmental Psychology,* 209-214.

Vanhamme, Joelle (2000), "The Link between Surprise and Satisfaction: Exploratory Research on how to Best Measure Surprise," *Journal of Marketing Management,* 16, 565-582.

Vohs, Kathleen D. and Todd F. Heatherton (2000), "Self-Regulatory Failure: A Resource-Depletion Approach," *Psychological Science,* 11 (May), 249-254.

---- (2000), "Some Perspectives on Positive Affect and Self-Regulation," *Psychological Inquiry,* 11, 184-187.

----Ronald Faber (2002), "Self-Regulation and Impulsive Spending Patterns," *Advances in Consumer Research,* 30, 125.

-----, Natalie J. Ciarocco, and Roy F. Baumeister (2005), "Self-Regulation and Self-Presentation: Regulatory Resource Depletion Impairs Impression Management and Efforful Self-Presentation Depletes Regulatory Resources," *Journal of Personality & Social Psychology,* 88 (4), 632-657.

----- (2006), "Self-Regulatory Resources Power the Reflective System: Evidence from Five Domains," *Journal of Consumer Psychology,* 16, 217-23.

Van Boven, L., and T. Gilovich (2003), "To Have or To Do? That is the Question," Journal of Personality and Social Psychology," 85 (6), 1192-1202.

Voss, Kevin E., Eric R. Spangenberg, and Bianca Grohmann (2003), "Measuring the Hedonic and Utilitarian Dimensions of Consumer Attitude," *Journal of Marketing Research,* 40 (August), 310-320.

Walther, Eva and Sofia Grigoriadis (2004), "Why Sad People Like Shoes Better: The Influence of Mood on the Evaluative Conditioning of Consumer Attitudes," *Psychology & Marketing,* 21 (October), 755-774.

Wansink, Brian and Michael L. Ray (1992), "Estimating an Advertisement's Impact on One's Consumption of a Brand," *Journal of Advertising Research,* 32 (May/June), 9-16.

Williams, Patti and Jennifer L. Aaker (2002), "Can Mixed Emotions Peacefully Coexist?" *Journal of Consumer Research,* 28 (March), 636-649.

Zaichkowsky, Judith L. (1985), "Measuring the Involvement Construct," *Journal of Consumer Research,* 12 (December), 341-352.

Zillman, Dolf (1988), "Mood Management through Communication Choices," *The American Behavioral Scientist),* 31 (January/February), 327-340.

APPENDIX A

Tables

TABLE 1

STUDY 1

Products: Gift Certificate for Groceries versus Gift Certificate for Dinner

Multivariate and Univariate Results

Independent Variables	ANCOVA Results		Univariate F Values		
	Wilks' Lambda	F Value	Attitude Towards Product	Purchase Intentions	Price Willing to Pay
Main Effects					
Emotions	0.94	2.00[c]	3.67[b]	3.00[b]	0.65
Cognitive Reappraisal	0.98	1.01	1.73	0.20	0.00
Interactions					
E X CR	0.94	2.18[c]	2.51	2.39[b]	0.89
Covariates					
Gender	0.98	1.25	0.07	1.47	2.62
Affect Intensity	0.92	6.48[b]	0.44	8.40[b]	0.10

a $p<.01$

b $p<.05$

c $p<.10$

117

TABLE 2

STUDY 1

Products: Gift Certificate for Groceries versus Gift Certificate for Dinner
Means

Hypothesis 1

EMOTIONS

	Amusement	Neutral	Sadness
Purchase Intentions	4.70	4.03	4.91
Attitudes	5.13	4.57	5.20
Price Willing to Pay	18.41	20.79	16.34

COGNITIVE REAPPRAISAL

	Low	High
Purchase Intentions	4.48	4.61
Attitudes	4.83	5.10
Price Willing to Pay	18.39	18.43

Hypothesis 2

EMOTIONS X COGNITIVE REAPPRAISAL (Purchase Intentions)

	Amusement	Neutral	Sadness
Low CR	4.49	3.71	5.25
High CR	4.92	4.35	4.58

EMOTIONS X COGNITIVE REAPPRAISAL (Attitude)

	Amusement	Neutral	Sadness
Low CR	5.07	4.12	5.32
High CR	5.16	5.01	5.17

EMOTIONS X COGNITIVE REAPPRAISAL (Price)

	Amusement	Neutral	Sadness
Low CR	16.68	19.9	18.60
High CR	20.00	20.97	14.30

TABLE 3

STUDY 1

**Products: Gift Certificate for Oil Change versus
Gift Certificate for On-line Music Downloading**

Multivariate and Univariate Results

Independent Variables	ANCOVA Results		Univariate F Values		
	Wilks' Lambda	F Value	Attitude Towards Product	Purchase Intentions	Price Willing to Pay
Main Effects					
Emotions	0.98	2.48[b]	0.38	0.89	5.14[b]
Cognitive Reappraisal	0.99	0.37	0.72	0.07	0.83
Interactions					
E X CR	0.98	0.68	1.20	0.15	0.93
Covariates					
Gender	0.95	2.46[c]	2.05	2.27	6.72[b]
Affect Intensity	0.96	1.78	2.46	0.25	0.52

a $p<.01$

b $p<.05$

c $p<.10$

119

TABLE 4

STUDY 1

**Products: Gift Certificate for Oil Change versus
Gift Certificate for On-line Music Downloading
Means**

Hypothesis 1

EMOTIONS

	Amusement	Neutral	Sadness
Purchase Intentions	4.10	4.30	3.96
Attitudes	4.30	4.60	4.46
Price Willing to Pay	13.31	6.56	6.87

COGNITIVE REAPPRAISAL

	Low	High
Purchase Intentions	4.09	4.15
Attitudes	4.37	4.56
Price Willing to Pay	9.79	8.04

Hypothesis 2

EMOTIONS X COGNITIVE REAPPRAISAL (Attitude)

	Amusement	Neutral	Sadness
Low CR	4.43	4.51	4.17
High CR	4.20	4.70	4.75

EMOTIONS X COGNITIVE REAPPRAISAL (Purchase Intentions)

	Amusement	Neutral	Sadness
Low CR	4.12	4.25	3.91
High CR	4.00	4.44	4.01

EMOTIONS X COGNITIVE REAPPRAISAL (Price)

	Amusement	Neutral	Sadness
Low CR	15.90	6.82	6.63
High CR	10.71	6.29	7.11

TABLE 5

STUDY 2

Multivariate and Univariate Results

Independent Variables	ANCOVA Results Wilks' Lambda	F Value	Attitude Toward Product	Desirability	Purchase Intentions	Level of Buying Impulse
Main Effects						
Ego Depletion	0.97	1.19	0.02	0.14	3.02^c	0.34
Emotions	0.88	2.82	0.81	0.59	9.60^b	0.49
Cognitive Reappraisal	0.99	0.47	0.01	0.01	0.01	1.56
Interactions						
Ego X Emotions	0.94	1.23	0.31	0.08	1.53^c	1.22
Ego X CR	0.98	0.68	0.01	0.39	0.16	1.15
Emotions X CR	0.93	1.48	0.85	0.15	3.20^b	1.50
Emotions X Ego X CR	0.98	0.42	0.60	0.51	0.14	0.63
Covariates						
Impulsivity	0.98	0.69	1.59	0.04	0.07	1.49
Eat to Regulate	0.99	0.55	0.10	1.09	0.42	1.26
Cheesecake	0.26	113^a	372^a	147^a	2.01	3.13^a

a p<.01
b p<.05
c p<.10

TABLE 6

STUDY 2

Means

Hypothesis 3

Buying Impulsiveness	
Ego Depletion	1.47
No-Ego Depletion	1.38

Hypothesis 4

Attitude Towards Product	
Ego Depletion	5.45
No-Ego Depletion	5.47

Desirability	
Ego Depletion	2.90
No-Ego Depletion	3.02

Purchase Intentions	
Ego Depletion	2.85
No-Ego Depletion	3.19

TABLE 7

STUDY 2

Hypothesis 5

Emotions X Ego Depletion for Attitude Toward Product

Contentment	
Ego Depletion	5.36
No-Ego Depletion	5.63
Neutral	
Ego Depletion	5.48
No-Ego Depletion	5.59
Fear/Anxiety	
Ego Depletion	5.52
No-Ego Depletion	5.20

Emotions X Ego Depletion for Purchase Intentions

Contentment	
Ego Depletion	2.80
No-Ego Depletion	3.57
Neutral	
Ego Depletion	2.45
No-Ego Depletion	2.41
Fear/Anxiety	
Ego Depletion	3.31
No-Ego Depletion	3.60

Emotions X Ego Depletion for Desirability

Contentment	
Ego Depletion	2.94
No-Ego Depletion	2.97
Neutral	
Ego Depletion	2.69
No-Ego Depletion	2.81
Fear/Anxiety	
Ego Depletion	3.08
No-Ego Depletion	3.29

TABLE 8

STUDY 2

Hypothesis 6

Emotions X Ego Depletion X Cognitive Reappraisal for Attitude Toward the Product	
Contentment (at Ego Depletion)	
Low Cognitive Reappraisal	5.24
High Cognitive Reappraisal	5.47
Neutral	
Low Cognitive Reappraisal	5.43
High Cognitive Reappraisal	5.54
Fear/Anxiety	
Low Cognitive Reappraisal	5.22
High Cognitive Reappraisal	5.83

Emotions X Ego Depletion X Cognitive Reapraisal for Desirability	
Contentment (at Ego Depletion)	
Low Cognitive Reappraisal	3.01
High Cognitive Reappraisal	2.81
Neutral	
Low Cognitive Reappraisal	2.65
High Cognitive Reappraisal	2.72
Fear/Anxiety	
Low Cognitive Reappraisal	2.98
High Cognitive Reappraisal	3.18

Emotions X Ego Depletion X Cognitive Reapraisal for Purchase Intentions	
Contentment (at Ego Depletion)	
Low Cognitive Reappraisal	3.10
High Cognitive Reappraisal	2.45
Neutral	
Low Cognitive Reappraisal	2.40
High Cognitive Reappraisal	2.51
Fear/Anxiety	
Low Cognitive Reappraisal	3.12
High Cognitive Reappraisal	3.51

TABLE 9

STUDY 3

	Ego Depletion	No Ego Depletion
Purchased Products	8	10

EGO DEPLETION

	Amusement	Sadness
Cookies	4	1

EGO DEPLETION X SADNESS (COOKIES)

Low Cognitive Reappraisers	0
High Cognitive Reappraisers	1

APPENDIX B

Figures

126

FIGURE 1

Projected Interaction and Planned Contrasts for H2

Similar patterns are expected for attitudes

Purchase Intentions

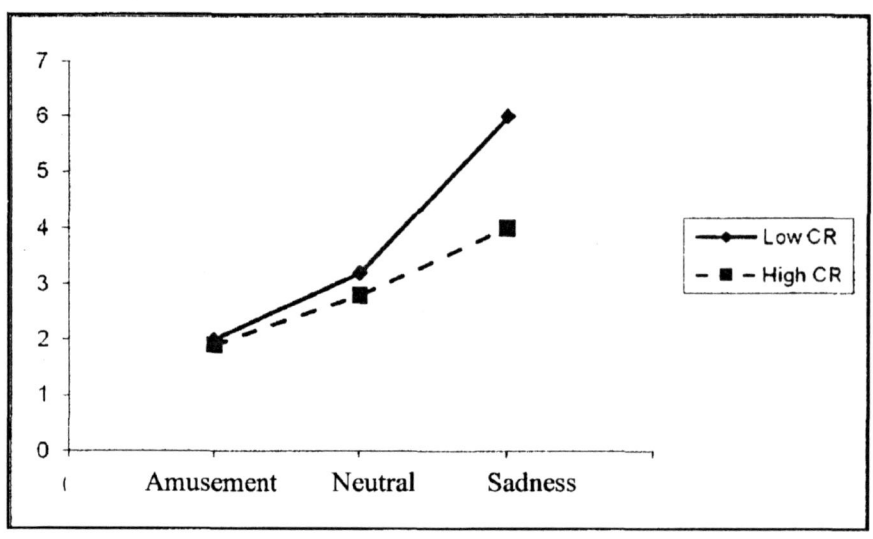

FIGURE 2

Projected Interaction and Planned Contrasts for H5

Similar patterns are expected for attitudes

Purchase Intentions

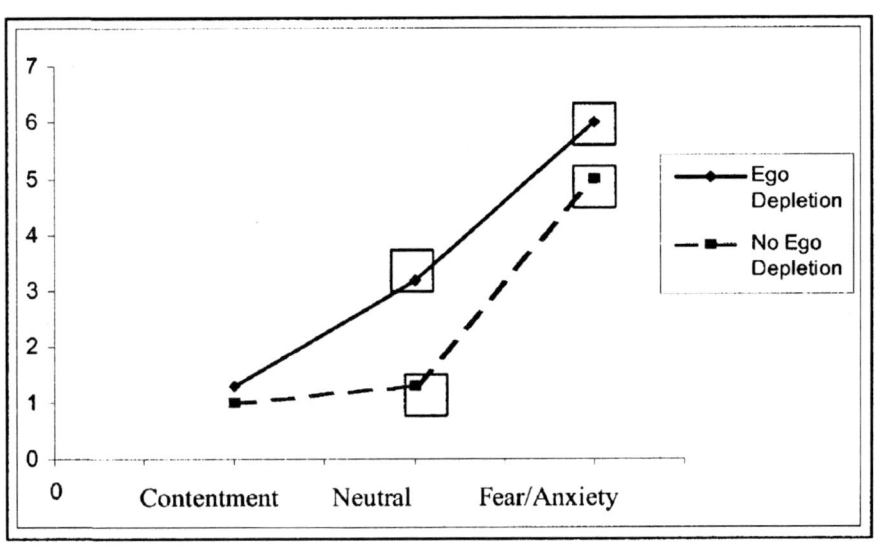

FIGURE 3

Projected Interaction and Planned Contrasts for H6

Similar patterns are expected for attitudes

Purchase Intentions at Ego Depletion

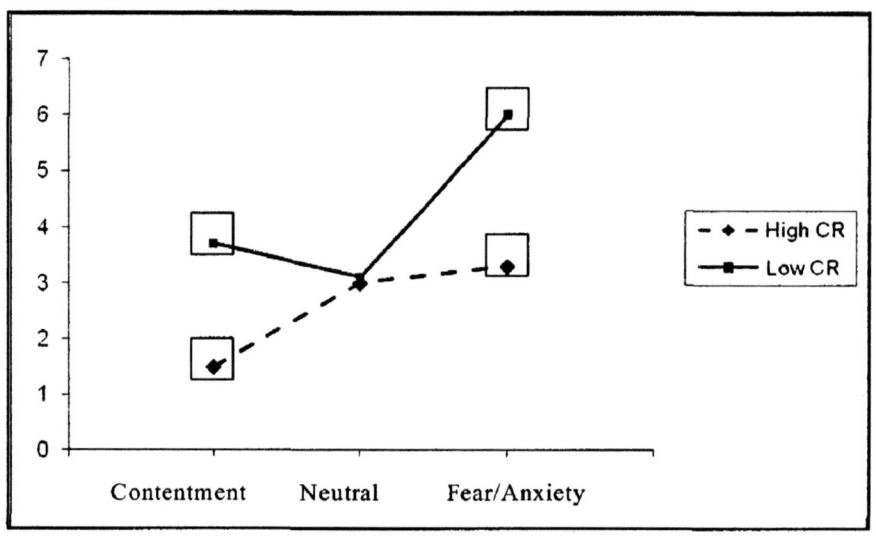

FIGURE 4

Hypothesis 1c

Emotions X Cognitive Reappraisal

Purchase Intentions

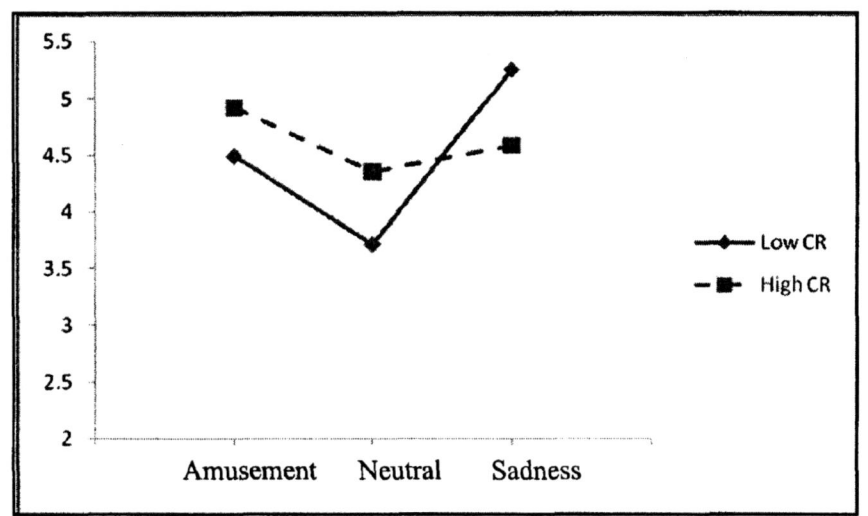

FIGURE 5

Hypothesis 5c

Ego Depletion X Emotions

Purchase Intentions

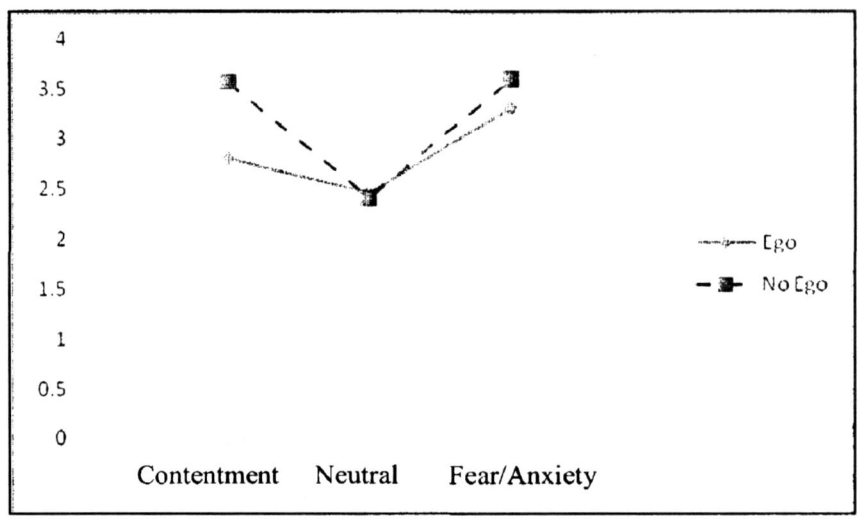

FIGURE 6

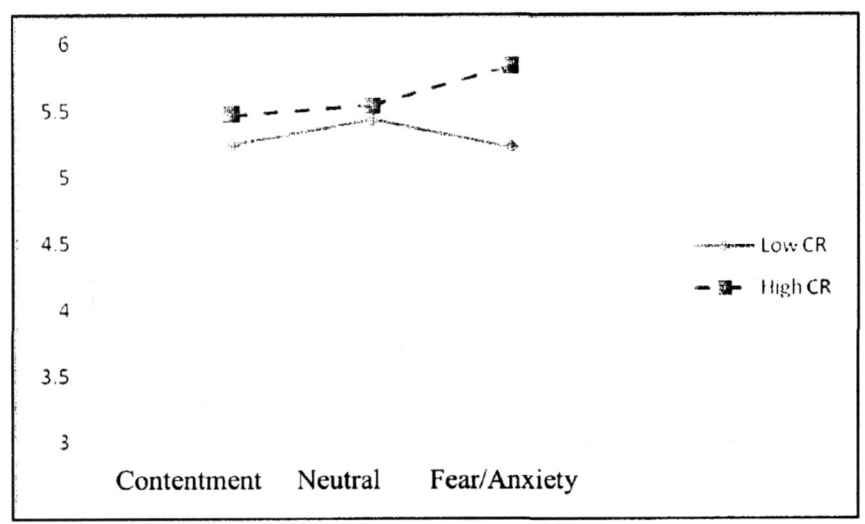

Hypothesis 6a

Emotions X Cognitive Reappraisal at Ego Depletion

Attitude toward the Product

FIGURE 7

Hypothesis 6c

Emotions X Cognitive Reappraisal at Ego Depletion

Purchase Intentions

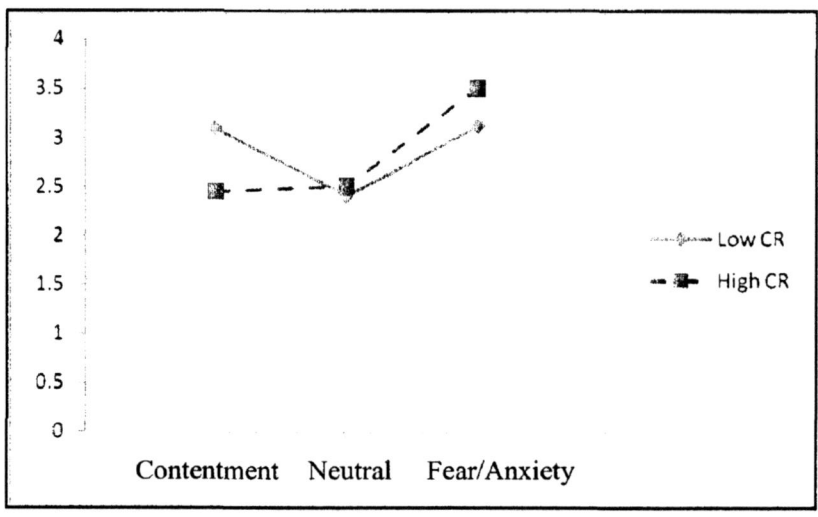

APPENDIX C

Survey Instruments

S T U D Y   1

This is a short study that will ask your feelings and

opinions about several issues. Please read each question very

carefully. Your opinions are very important to our research, so please take

your time and answer questions to the best of your ability.

INFORMED CONSENT

Your identity will be kept confidential and your name will not be used in any report. Your

participation in this study is completely voluntary. There is no penalty for not partici-

pating. You have the right to withdraw from the study at anytime without conse-

quence. By signing your name below, you agree that you have read the procedure

described above and voluntarily agree to participate.

Signature: _____

Name (print): _____

In what year were you born? _____

What is your gender?   **Male**   **Female**

PLEASE READ THE FOLLOWING CAREFULLY.

Imagine that you have an opportunity to bid on several items in a silent auction. One item is a $35 gift certificate for groceries at a local supermarket and the other is a $35 gift certificate for dinner with friends at a local restaurant.

Please indicate your relative preference for each item at the present moment on the scales that follow below.

It is likely that I will purchase the **gift certificate for groceries.**	1 2 3 4 5 6 7	It is likely that I will purchase the **gift certificate for dinner.**
It is probable that I will purchase the **gift certificate for groceries.**	1 2 3 4 5 6 7	It is possible that I will purchase the **gift certificate for dinner.**
It is possible that I will purchase the **gift certificate for groceries.**	1 2 3 4 5 6 7	It is probable that I will purchase the **gift certificate for dinner.**
It is certain that I will purchase the **gift certificate for groceries.**	1 2 3 4 5 6 7	It is certain that I will purchase the **gift certificate for dinner.**
I definitely will purchase the **gift certificate for groceries.**	1 2 3 4 5 6 7	I definitely will purchase the **gift certificate for dinner.**

. . . .

The **gift certificate for groceries** sounds good.	1 2 3 4 5 6 7	The **gift certificate for dinner** sounds good.
The **gift certificate for groceries** sounds desirable.	1 2 3 4 5 6 7	The **gift certificate for dinner** sounds desirable.
The **gift certificate for groceries** sounds appealing.	1 2 3 4 5 6 7	The **gift certificate for dinner** sounds appealing.
The **gift certificate for groceries** sounds favorable.	1 2 3 4 5 6 7	The **gift certificate for dinner** sounds favorable.

If given the opportunity to place a bid, the most I would pay for the **gift certificate for groceries** is $_____.

If given the opportunity to place a bid, the most I would pay for the **gift certificate for dinner** is $_____.

• •

Please indicate how you feel about each item at the present moment on the scales that follow below.

The **gift certificate for groceries** is important to me.	1 2 3 4 5 6 7	The **gift certificate for dinner** is important to me.
The **gift certificate for groceries** is of concern to me.	1 2 3 4 5 6 7	The **gift certificate for dinner** is of concern to me.
The **gift certificate for groceries** means a lot to me.	1 2 3 4 5 6 7	The **gift certificate for dinner** means a lot to me.
The **gift certificate for groceries** matters to me.	1 2 3 4 5 6 7	The **gift certificate for dinner** matters to me.
The **gift certificate for groceries** is significant to me.	1 2 3 4 5 6 7	The **gift certificate for dinner** is significant to me.
The **gift certificate for groceries** is trivial to me.	1 2 3 4 5 6 7	The **gift certificate for dinner** is trivial to me.
The **gift certificate for groceries** is vital to me.	1 2 3 4 5 6 7	The **gift certificate for dinner** is vital to me.

YOU CAN NOW PLACE YOUR BID IN ACTUAL CASH!

Below please indicate how much you would pay for the gift certificate for groceries and the gift certificate for dinner. **THE HIGHEST BIDDERS WILL ACTUALLY RECEIVE THE GIFT CERTIFICATES; HOWEVER, EACH BIDDER MUST BE PREPARED TO EXCHANGE THE ACTUAL BID AMOUNT IN US DOLLARS FOR THE CERTIFICATE ON MAY 4TH. THE SUPERMARKET AND RESTAURANT ARE LOCATED IN THE FAYET-TEVILLE AREA AND WILL NOT BE DISCLOSED UNTIL EVERYONE HAS COMPLETED THIS SURVEY, BUT BOTH CERTIFICATES ARE VALUED AT $35.**

I am bidding $_____ (actual US dollars) for the gift certificate for groceries at a local (in the Fayetteville area) supermarket.

I am bidding $_____ (actual US dollars) for the gift certificate for dinner at a local (in the Fayetteville area) restaurant.

WINNERS WILL BE CONTACTED NEXT WEEK ON MAY 4TH. PLEASE LEAVE YOUR CONTACT INFORMATION BELOW (CELL PHONE, EMAIL ETC).

CONTACT INFORMATION   _____

_____

PLEASE ANSWER THE FOLLOWING ACCORDING TO THE WAY YOU FELT WHILE VIEWING THE FILM.

	Do not feel the emotion the slightest bit								I feel this emotion very strongly
I feel **amusement**...	1	2	3	4	5	6	7	8	9
I feel **anger**...	1	2	3	4	5	6	7	8	9
I feel **anxiety**...	1	2	3	4	5	6	7	8	9
I feel **contentment**...	1	2	3	4	5	6	7	8	9
I feel **disgust**...	1	2	3	4	5	6	7	8	9
I feel **fearful**..	1	2	3	4	5	6	7	8	9
I feel **sad**...	1	2	3	4	5	6	7	8	9
I feel **surprised**...	1	2	3	4	5	6	7	8	9
I feel **good**...	1	2	3	4	5	6	7	8	9
I feel **bad** ...	1	2	3	4	5	6	7	8	9

Had you seen the film you viewed before? _____ No _____ Yes

Did you close your eyes or look away during any of the scenes _____No _____Yes

I watched the film carefully.

Strongly Disagree								Strongly Agree
1	2	3	4	5	6	7	8	9

BELOW ARE SOME QUESTIONS ABOUT YOUR EMOTIONAL LIFE, IN PARTICULAR, HOW YOU CONTROL (THAT IS, REGULATE AND MANAGE) YOUR EMOTIONS.

FOR EACH ITEM, PLEASE ANSWER USING THE FOLLOWING SCALE:

Strongly
Disagree

Strongly
Agree

1----------2----------3----------4----------5----------6----------7

1. _____ When I want to feel more positive emotion (such as joy or amusement), I change what I'm thinking about.

2. _____ I keep my emotions to myself.

3. _____ When I want to feel less negative emotion (such as sadness or anger), I change what I'm thinking about.

4. _____ When I am feeling positive emotions, I am careful not to express them.

5. _____ When I'm faced with a stressful situation, I make myself think about it in a way that helps me stay calm.

6. _____ I control my emotions by not expressing them.

7. _____ When I want to feel more positive emotion, I change the way I'm thinking about the situation.

8. _____ I control my emotions by changing the way I think about the situation I'm in.

9. _____ When I am feeling negative emotions, I make sure not to express them.

10. _____ When I want to feel less negative emotion, I change the way I'm thinking about the situation.

****

PLEASE CIRCLE THE NUMBER NEXT TO THE STATEMENT THAT BEST DESCRIBES YOU.

1) In general, I consider myself to be a fun-loving person.

2) In general, I consider myself to be a responsible person.

3) Both of the above are equally important to me.

THE FOLLOWING QUESTIONS REFER TO EMOTIONAL REACTIONS TO TYPICAL LIFE EVENTS. PLEASE INDICATE HOW YOU REACT TO THESE EVENTS BY PLACING A NUMBER FROM THE FOLLOWING SCALE IN THE BLANK SPACE PRECEDING EACH ITEM. PLEASE BASE YOUR ANSWERS ON HOW YOU REACT, NOT ON HOW YOU THINK OTHERS REACT OR HOW YOU THINK A PERSON SHOULD REACT.

Never	Almost Never	Occasionally	Usually	Almost Always	Always
1 ————	2 ——————	3 ————	4 ——————	5 ———————	6

1. _____ When I accomplish something difficult, I feel delighted or elated.

2. _____ When I feel happy, it is a strong type of exuberance.

3. _____ I enjoy being with other people very much.

4. _____ I fell pretty bad when I tell a lie.

5. _____ When I solve a small personal problem, I feel euphoric.

6. _____ My emotions tend to be more intense than those of most people.

7. _____ My happy moods are so strong that I feel like I'm "in heaven."

8. _____ I get overly enthusiastic.

9. _____ If I complete a task I thought was impossible, I am ecstatic.

10. _____ My heart races at the anticipation of some exciting event.

11. _____ Sad movies deeply touch me.

12. _____ When I'm happy, it's a feeling of being untroubled and content rather than being zestful and aroused.

13. _____ When I talk in front of a group for the first time, my voice gets shaky and my heart races.

14. _____ When something good happens, I am usually much more jubilant than others.

15. _____ My friends might say I'm emotional.

16. _____ The memories I like the most are of those times when I felt content and peaceful rather than zestful and enthusiastic.

17. _____ The sight of someone who is hurt badly affects me strongly.

18. _____ When I'm feeling well, it's easy for me to go from being in a good mood to being really joyful.

19. _____ "Calm and cool" could easily describe me.

20. _____ When I'm happy, I feel like I'm bursting with joy.

21. _____ Seeing a picture of some violent car accident in a newspaper makes me feel sick to my stomach.

141

IN THE FOLLOWING SECTION, PLEASE BE AS HONEST AND ACCURATE AS YOU CAN. TRY NOT TO LET YOUR RESPONSE TO ONE STATEMENT INFLUENCE YOUR RESPONSES TO OTHER STATEMENTS. THERE ARE NO "CORRECT" OR "INCORRECT" ANSWERS. ANSWER ACCORDING TO YOUR OWN FEELINGS, RATHER THAN HOW YOU THINK "MOST PEOPLE" WOULD ANSWER.

	Strongly Disagree				Strongly Agree
In uncertain times, I usually expect the best.	1	2	3	4	5
If something can go wrong for me, it will.	1	2	3	4	5
I'm always optimistic about my future.	1	2	3	4	5
I hardly ever expect things to go my way.	1	2	3	4	5
I rarely count on good things happening to me.	1	2	3	4	5
Overall, I expect more good things to happen to me than bad.	1	2	3	4	5

THANK YOU FOR YOUR TIME!

S T U D Y   2

This is a short study that will ask your feelings and opinions about several issues. Please read each question very carefully. Your opinions are very important to our research, so please take your time and answer questions to the best of your ability.

INFORMED CONSENT

Your identity will be kept confidential and your name will not be used in any report. Your participation in this study is completely voluntary. There is no penalty for not participating. You have the right to withdraw from the study at anytime without consequence. By signing your name below, you agree that you have read the procedure described above and voluntarily agree to participate.

Signature: _____

Name (print):   _____

In what year were you born? _____

What is your gender?   **Male**   **Female**

T h a n k   Y o u !

The exercise below assesses your ability to attend to detail. In the passage below, please cross out the letter "e" when it appears in the passage. However, if the "e" is adjacent to another vowel or one letter away from a vowel, do not cross it out.

Example: ~~E~~dmond ~~e~~njoys sleeping and mundane activities.

Assuming sphericity, power calculations are conducted as for other designs (Keele, 196?). For example, in Section 13.2.3, Cohen's f was calculated as .52 for the depression data of Table 13.1. Using GPOWER, we select "Other F Tests" and then enter the values of f, numerator and denominator df, and α. The result is .48, the power of the test of the Seasons source of variance. The noncentrality parameter, λ, equals Nf^2, or 6.10. Using the UCLA calculator, we enter the F needed for significance at the .05 level with 3 and 9 df, the numerator and denominator df, and λ. The critical F is 2.845 and $\lambda = 6.10$. The calculator returns β, the Type 2 error probability. This value is .52 and, subtracting from 1, we again have the power, .48.

Ego Depletion Condition

The exercise below assesses your ability to attend to detail. In the passage below, please cross out the letter "e'" when it appears in the passage.

Example: ~~E~~dmond ~~e~~njoys sl~~ee~~ping and mundan~~e~~ activiti~~e~~s.

Assuming sphericity, power calculations are conducted as for other designs (Koele, 1982). For example, in Section 13.2.3, Cohen's f was calculated as .33 for the depression data of Table 13.1. Using GPOWER, we select "Other F Tests" and then enter the values of f^2, numerator and denominator df, and α. The result is .48, the power of the test of the Seasons source of variance. The noncentrality parameter, λ, equals Nf^2, or 6.10. Using the UCLA calculator, we enter the F needed for significance at the .05 level with 3 and 39 df, the numerator and denominator df, and λ. The critical F is 2.845 and $\lambda = 6.10$. The calculator returns β, the Type 2 error probability. This value is .52 and, subtracting from 1, we again have the power, .48.

Control Condition

PLEASE READ THE FOLLOWING CAREFULLY. TRY TO IMAGINE YOURSELF IN THE SCENARIO AND HOW YOU MIGHT REACT. THERE ARE NO RIGHT OR WRONG ANSWERS TO THE QUESTIONS.

Imagine that you are a college student with a part-time job. In three-days, you will get your paycheck, but until then you only have $20 left for food and necessities. You go to Lagasse's Market to buy some needed groceries, and see a display for a decadent bakery-style cheesecake. The cheesecake costs $12 and would be great to share with friends.

The probability that I would purchase the creamy cheesecake is:

Unlikely _ _ _ _ _ _ _ Likely

Nonexistent _ _ _ _ _ _ _ Existent

Improbable_ _ _ _ _ _ _ Probable

Impossible _ _ _ _ _ _ _ Possible

Uncertain _ _ _ _ _ _ _ Certain

Definitely Would _ _ _ _ _ _ _ Definitely Would Not

A creamy cheesecake sounds:

Good _ _ _ _ _ _ _ Bad

Tasteful_ _ _ _ _ _ _ Not tasteful

Desirable _ _ _ _ _ _ _ Undesirable

Appealing _ _ _ _ _ _ _ Unappealing

Appetizing _ _ _ _ _ _ _ Unappetizing

Favorable _ _ _ _ _ _ _ Unfavorable

Buying the creamy cheesecake is:

Important to me _ _ _ _ _ _ _ Unimportant to me

Of no concern to me _ _ _ _ _ _ _ Of concern to me

Means a lot to me _ _ _ _ _ _ _ Means nothing to me

Matters to me _ _ _ _ _ _ _ Doesn't matter to me

Significant to me _ _ _ _ _ _ _ Insignificant to me

Trivial to me _ _ _ _ _ _ _ Fundamental to me

Vital to me_ _ _ _ _ _ _ Superfluous to me

	Strongly Disagree						Strongly Agree
I have an urge for the cheesecake.	1	2	3	4	5	6	7
I have a desire for the cheesecake.	1	2	3	4	5	6	7
I have a longing for the cheesecake.	1	2	3	4	5	6	7

Please indicate your likelihood of buying the cheesecake on a scale of 0 to 100 where 0 = definitely will not buy and 100 = definitely will buy.

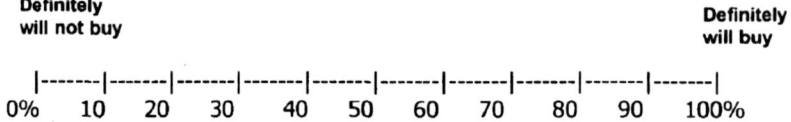

Definitely
will not buy

Definitely
will buy

|-------|-------|-------|-------|-------|-------|-------|-------|-------|-------|-------|
0%   10   20   30   40   50   60   70   80   90   100%

If you had the option, which of the following purchase alternatives would *you* make:

1) buy needed staple groceries only

2) want the cheesecake but not buy it

3) decide not to buy all the staple groceries needed to have money for the cheesecake

4) buy both the groceries needed and the cheesecake with a credit card

5) buy all the groceries needed, cheesecake, and some strawberry topping for the

cheese cake with a credit card.

Now, in your opinion, which of the following purchase alternatives would the *typical person* make:

1) buy needed staple groceries only

2) want the cheesecake but not buy it

3) decide not to buy all the staple groceries needed to have money for the cheesecake

4) buy both the groceries needed and the cheesecake with a credit card

5) buy all the groceries needed, cheesecake, and some strawberry topping for the

cheese cake with a credit card.

PLEASE ANSWER THE FOLLOWING ACCORDING TO THE WAY YOU FELT WHILE VIEWING THE FILM.

	Do not feel the emotion the slightest bit							I feel this emotion very strongly	
I feel **amusement**...	1	2	3	4	5	6	7	8	9
I feel **anger**...	1	2	3	4	5	6	7	8	9
I feel **anxiety**...	1	2	3	4	5	6	7	8	9
I feel **contentment**...	1	2	3	4	5	6	7	8	9
I feel **disgust**...	1	2	3	4	5	6	7	8	9
I feel **fearful**..	1	2	3	4	5	6	7	8	9
I feel **sad**...	1	2	3	4	5	6	7	8	9
I feel **surprised**...	1	2	3	4	5	6	7	8	9
I feel **good**...	1	2	3	4	5	6	7	8	9
I feel **bad** ...	1	2	3	4	5	6	7	8	9

Had you seen the film you viewed before?   _____ No   _____ Yes

Did you close your eyes or look away during any of the scenes   _____No
_____Yes

I watched the film carefully.

	Strongly Disagree							Strongly Agree	
	1	2	3	4	5	6	7	8	9

BELOW ARE SOME QUESTIONS ABOUT YOUR EMOTIONAL LIFE, IN PARTICULAR, HOW YOU CONTROL (THAT IS, REGULATE AND MANAGE) YOUR EMOTIONS.

FOR EACH ITEM, PLEASE ANSWER USING THE FOLLOWING SCALE:

Strongly   Strongly
Disagree   Agree

1----------2-----------3-----------4-----------5-----------6-----------7

1. _____   When I want to feel more positive emotion (such as joy or amusement), I change what I'm thinking about.

2. _____   I keep my emotions to myself.

3. _____   When I want to feel less negative emotion (such as sadness or anger), I change what I'm thinking about.

4. _____   When I am feeling positive emotions, I am careful not to express them.

5. _____   When I'm faced with a stressful situation, I make myself think about it in a way that helps me stay calm.

6. _____   I control my emotions by not expressing them.

7. _____   When I want to feel more positive emotion, I change the way I'm thinking about the situation.

8. _____   I control my emotions by changing the way I think about the situation I'm in.

9. _____   When I am feeling negative emotions, I make sure not to express them.

10. _____   When I want to feel less negative emotion, I change the way I'm thinking about the situation.

****

PLEASE CIRCLE THE NUMBER NEXT TO THE STATEMENT THAT BEST DESCRIBES YOU.

1)   In general, I consider myself to be a fun-loving person.

2)   In general, I consider myself to be a responsible person.

3)   Both of the above are equally important to me.

THE FOLLOWING QUESTIONS REFER TO EMOTIONAL REACTIONS TO TYPICAL LIFE EVENTS. PLEASE INDICATE HOW YOU REACT TO THESE EVENTS BY PLACING A NUMBER FROM THE FOLLOWING SCALE IN THE BLANK SPACE PRECEDING EACH ITEM. PLEASE BASE YOUR ANSWERS ON HOW YOU REACT, NOT ON HOW YOU THINK OTHERS REACT OR HOW YOU THINK A PERSON SHOULD REACT.

Never	Almost Never	Occasionally	Usually	Almost Always	Always
1	2	3	4	5	6

1. _____ When I accomplish something difficult, I feel delighted or elated.

2. _____ When I feel happy, it is a strong type of exuberance.

3. _____ I enjoy being with other people very much.

4. _____ I fell pretty bad when I tell a lie.

5. _____ When I solve a small personal problem, I feel euphoric.

6. _____ My emotions tend to be more intense than those of most people.

7. _____ My happy moods are so strong that I feel like I'm "in heaven."

8. _____ I get overly enthusiastic.

9. _____ If I complete a task I thought was impossible, I am ecstatic.

10. _____ My heart races at the anticipation of some exciting event.

11. _____ Sad movies deeply touch me.

12. _____ When I'm happy, it's a feeling of being untroubled and content rather than being zestful and aroused.

13. _____ When I talk in front of a group for the first time, my voice gets shaky and my heart races.

14. _____ When something good happens, I am usually much more jubilant than others.

15. _____ My friends might say I'm emotional.

16. _____ The memories I like the most are of those times when I felt content and peaceful rather than zestful and enthusiastic.

17. _____ The sight of someone who is hurt badly affects me strongly.

18. _____ When I'm feeling well, it's easy for me to go from being in a good mood to being really joyful.

19. _____ "Calm and cool" could easily describe me.

20. _____ When I'm happy, I feel like I'm bursting with joy.

21. _____ Seeing a picture of some violent car accident in a newspaper makes me feel sick to my stomach.

IN THE FOLLOWING SECTION, PLEASE BE AS HONEST AND ACCURATE AS YOU CAN. TRY NOT TO LET YOUR RESPONSE TO ONE STATEMENT INFLUENCE YOUR RESPONSES TO OTHER STATEMENTS.

	Strongly Disagree				Strongly Agree
In uncertain times, I usually expect the best.	1	2	3	4	5
If something can go wrong for me, it will.	1	2	3	4	5
I'm always optimistic about my future.	1	2	3	4	5
I hardly ever expect things to go my way.	1	2	3	4	5
I rarely count on good things happening to me.	1	2	3	4	5
Overall, I expect more good things to happen to me than bad.	1	2	3	4	5

PLEASE ANSWER THE FOLLOWING TO THE BEST OF YOUR ABILITY.

	Strongly Disagree						Strongly Agree
I feel like I had to concentrate a great deal in order to accomplish the task (crossing out the letter "e'") at the beginning of this survey.	1	2	3	4	5	6	7
Completing the task at the beginning of this survey (requiring me to cross out the letter "e") was difficult.	1	2	3	4	5	6	7
The task at the beginning of this survey (crossing out the letter "e") required some effort.	1	2	3	4	5	6	7
I like cheesecake.	1	2	3	4	5	6	7

READ EACH OF THE FOLLOWING ADJECTIVES CAREFULLY AND INDICATE HOW WELL THEY WOULD DESCRIBE YOU. CIRCLE THE NUMBER ON THE SCALE NEXT TO EACH ADJECTIVE.

	Strongly Disagree						Strongly Agree
Impulsive	1	2	3	4	5	6	7
Careless	1	2	3	4	5	6	7
Self-controlled	1	2	3	4	5	6	7
Extravagant	1	2	3	4	5	6	7
Farsighted	1	2	3	4	5	6	7
Responsible	1	2	3	4	5	6	7
Restrained	1	2	3	4	5	6	7
Easily Tempted	1	2	3	4	5	6	7
Rational	1	2	3	4	5	6	7
Methodical	1	2	3	4	5	6	7
Enjoy Spending	1	2	3	4	5	6	7
A Planner	1	2	3	4	5	6	7

PLEASE ANSWER THE FOLLOWING QUESTIONS. FOR EACH ITEM, PLEASE ANSWER USING THE SCALE PROVIDED.

	Never						Very Frequently
I eat to cheer myself up when I am feeling bad.	1	2	3	4	5	6	7
When I am feeling bad, I eat something.	1	2	3	4	5	6	7
Eating something helps me to cope with feeling bad.	1	2	3	4	5	6	7

THANK YOU FOR YOUR TIME!

S T U D Y   3

This is a short study that will ask your feelings and opinions about several issues. Please read each question very carefully. Your opinions are very important to our research, so please take your time and answer questions to the best of your ability.

INFORMED CONSENT

Your identity will be kept confidential and your name will not be used in any report. Your

participation in this study is completely voluntary. There is no penalty for not participating. You have the right to withdraw from the study at anytime without consequence. By signing your name below, you agree that you have read the procedure described above and voluntarily agree to participate.

Signature: _____

Name (print):   _____

In what year were you born? _____

What is your gender?   Male   Female

T h a n k   Y o u !

Below (and on the back of this sheet of paper if needed), please list all your thoughts. However, in listing your thoughts, please try not to think about a WHITE BEAR. If you do think about a WHITE BEAR, please place a checkmark in the box below everytime you think about a WHITE BEAR. Please do not worry about punctuation or grammar. Your thoughts will not be shared with anyone else.

Ego Depletion Condition

Below (and on the back of this sheet of paper if needed), please list all your thoughts. Other participants have been asked to restrict specific thoughts (such as thinking about a white bear), however, please list anything you think about. Do not worry about punctuation or grammar. Your thoughts will not be shared with anyone else.

Control Condition

BELOW ARE SOME QUESTIONS ABOUT YOUR EMOTIONAL LIFE, IN PARTICULAR, HOW YOU CONTROL (THAT IS, REGULATE AND MANAGE) YOUR EMOTIONS.

FOR EACH ITEM, PLEASE ANSWER USING THE FOLLOWING SCALE:

Strongly
Disagree

Strongly
Agree

1----------2-----------3-----------4-----------5-----------6-----------7

1. _____ When I want to feel more positive emotion (such as joy or amusement), I change what I'm thinking about.

2. _____ I keep my emotions to myself.

3. _____ When I want to feel less negative emotion (such as sadness or anger), I change what I'm thinking about.

4. _____ When I am feeling positive emotions, I am careful not to express them.

5. _____ When I'm faced with a stressful situation, I make myself think about it in a way that helps me stay calm.

6. _____ I control my emotions by not expressing them.

7. _____ When I want to feel more positive emotion, I change the way I'm thinking about the situation.

8. _____ I control my emotions by changing the way I think about the situation I'm in.

9. _____ When I am feeling negative emotions, I make sure not to express them.

10. _____ When I want to feel less negative emotion, I change the way I'm thinking about the situation.

156

PLEASE STOP AND WAIT FOR INSTRUCTIONS

QTY

___ **Fruit Pack**

___ **Cookies**

___ **None**

PLEASE ANSWER THE FOLLOWING TO THE BEST OF YOUR ABILITY.

	Strongly Disagree	I was tempted to buy something. 1					Strongly Agree
2	3	4	5	6	7		

	Strongly Disagree						Strongly Agree
I was tempted to buy the fruit pack.	1	2	3	4	5	6	7
I was tempted to buy the cookies.	1	2	3	4	5	6	7
I like bananas.	1	2	3	4	5	6	7
I like apples.	1	2	3	4	5	6	7
I like cookies.	1	2	3	4	5	6	7

Please explain **why, or why you did not** purchase something?

PLEASE ANSWER THE FOLLOWING TO THE BEST OF YOUR ABILITY.

	Strongly Disagree						Strongly Agree
The task at the beginning of this survey (listing my thoughts) required some effort.	1	2	3	4	5	6	7

Listing my thoughts made me feel...

	Strongly Disagree						Strongly Agree
Tired.	1	2	3	4	5	6	7
Worn-out.	1	2	3	4	5	6	7
Thoughtful.	1	2	3	4	5	6	7
Excited.	1	2	3	4	5	6	7
Happy.	1	2	3	4	5	6	7
Sad.	1	2	3	4	5	6	7
Angry.	1	2	3	4	5	6	7
Calm.	1	2	3	4	5	6	7

PLEASE ANSWER THE FOLLOWING ACCORDING TO THE WAY YOU FELT WHILE VIEWING THE FILM.

	Do not feel the emotion the slightest bit								I feel this emotion very strongly
I felt **amusement**...	1	2	3	4	5	6	7	8	9
I felt **sad**...	1	2	3	4	5	6	7	8	9
I felt **good**...	1	2	3	4	5	6	7	8	9
I felt **bad** ...	1	2	3	4	5	6	7	8	9

Had you seen the film you viewed before? _____ No _____ Yes

Did you close your eyes or look away during any of the scenes _____ No _____ Yes

I watched the film carefully.

Strongly Disagree								Strongly Agree
1	2	3	4	5	6	7	8	9

****

READ EACH OF THE FOLLOWING ADJECTIVES CAREFULLY AND INDICATE HOW WELL THEY DESCRIBE YOU. CIRCLE THE NUMBER ON THE SCALE NEXT TO EACH ADJECTIVE.

	Strongly Disagree						Strongly Agree
Impulsive	1	2	3	4	5	6	7
Enjoy Spending	1	2	3	4	5	6	7
Easily Tempted	1	2	3	4	5	6	7
Enjoy Spending	1	2	3	4	5	6	7

THANK YOU FOR YOUR TIME!

FOLLOW-UP STUDY

This is a short study that will ask your feelings and opinions about several issues. Please read each question very carefully. Your opinions are very important to our research, so please take your time and answer questions to the best of your ability.

INFORMED CONSENT

Your identity will be kept confidential and your name will not be used in any report. Your participation in this study is completely voluntary. There is no penalty for not participating. You have the right to withdraw from the study at anytime without consequence. By signing your name below, you agree that you have read the procedure described above and voluntarily agree to participate.

Signature: _____

Name (print): _____

In what year were you born? _____

What is your gender?   **Male**   **Female**

Thank You!

Below (and on the back of this sheet of paper if needed), please list all your thoughts. However, in listing your thoughts, please try not to think about a WHITE BEAR. If you do think about a WHITE BEAR, please place a checkmark in the box below everytime you think about a WHITE BEAR. Please do not worry about punctuation or grammar. Your thoughts will not be shared with anyone else.

Ego Depletion Condition

Below (and on the back of this sheet of paper if needed), please list all your thoughts. Other participants have been asked to restrict specific thoughts (such as thinking about a white bear), however, please list anything you think about. Do not worry about punctuation or grammar. Your thoughts will not be shared with anyone else.

Control Condition

IMAGINE YOURSELF IN THE FOLLOWING SCENARIO.

One day, you go for a walk to get some fresh air. It is a nice day out, but no one is out on the street. You see two dollars lying on the street, and since their is no evidence that It belongs to anyone, you pick it up and put it in your pocket.

Further down the street, you come upon a snack bar and the following items are available for sale. Please indicate by CIRCLING THE ITEM whether you would purchase the item. You do not have to purchase any items or you may purchase as many items as you like.

Granola Bar @ $.75   Bag of Pretzels @ $.75

Chocolate Bar @ $.75   Bag of Doritos @ $.75

A Bottle of Orange Juice @1.25   A Plain Bagel @ $1.25

A Coke @ $1.25   A Donut @ $1.25

****

PLEASE ANSWER THE FOLLOWING TO THE BEST OF YOUR ABILITY.

	Strongly Disagree						Strongly Agree
If I found two dollars on the street now, I would be tempted to buy something.	1	2	3	4	5	6	7
If I found two dollars on the street now, I would have a strong urge to buy something.	1	2	3	4	5	6	7
I would have the desire to purchase something if I found two dollars on the street right now.	1	2	3	4	5	6	7

163

PLEASE ANSWER THE FOLLOWING TO THE BEST OF YOUR ABILITY.

I feel like I had to concentrate a great deal in order to perform the task at the beginning of this survey where I listed my thoughts.	1 2 3 4 5 6 7
Listing my thoughts at the beginning of this survey was difficult.	1 2 3 4 5 6 7
The task at the beginning of this survey (listing my thoughts) required some effort.	1 2 3 4 5 6 7

After listing my thoughts at the beginning of the survey...

I felt tired.	1 2 3 4 5 6 7
I felt worn-out	1 2 3 4 5 6 7
I felt thoughtful.	1 2 3 4 5 6 7
I felt excited.	1 2 3 4 5 6 7
I felt happy.	1 2 3 4 5 6 7
I felt sad.	1 2 3 4 5 6 7
I felt angry.	1 2 3 4 5 6 7
I felt calm.	1 2 3 4 5 6 7

BELOW ARE SOME QUESTIONS ABOUT YOUR EMOTIONAL LIFE, IN PARTICULAR, HOW YOU CONTROL (THAT IS, REGULATE AND MANAGE) YOUR EMOTIONS.

FOR EACH ITEM, PLEASE ANSWER USING THE FOLLOWING SCALE:

Strongly Disagree   Strongly Agree

1----------2----------3----------4----------5----------6----------7

1. _____ When I want to feel more positive emotion (such as joy or amusement), I change what I'm thinking about.

2. _____ I keep my emotions to myself.

3. _____ When I want to feel less negative emotion (such as sadness or anger), I change what I'm thinking about.

4. _____ When I am feeling positive emotions, I am careful not to express them.

5. _____ When I'm faced with a stressful situation, I make myself think about it in a way that helps me stay calm.

6. _____ I control my emotions by not expressing them.

7. _____ When I want to feel more positive emotion, I change the way I'm thinking about the situation.

8. _____ I control my emotions by changing the way I think about the situation I'm in.

9. _____ When I am feeling negative emotions, I make sure not to express them.

10. _____ When I want to feel less negative emotion, I change the way I'm thinking about the situation.

PLEASE ANSWER THE FOLLOWING ACCORDING TO THE WAY YOU FELT WHILE VIEWING THE FILM.

	Do not feel the emotion the slightest bit								**I feel this emotion very strongly**
I felt **amusement**...	1	2	3	4	5	6	7	8	9
I felt **sad**...	1	2	3	4	5	6	7	8	9
I felt **good**...	1	2	3	4	5	6	7	8	9
I felt **bad** ...	1	2	3	4	5	6	7	8	9

****

READ EACH OF THE FOLLOWING ADJECTIVES CAREFULLY AND INDICATE HOW WELL THEY DESCRIBE YOU. CIRCLE THE NUMBER ON THE SCALE NEXT TO EACH ADJECTIVE.

	Strongly Disagree						**Strongly Agree**
Impulsive	1	2	3	4	5	6	7
Careless	1	2	3	4	5	6	7
Self-controlled	1	2	3	4	5	6	7
Extravagant	1	2	3	4	5	6	7
Farsighted	1	2	3	4	5	6	7
Responsible	1	2	3	4	5	6	7
Restrained	1	2	3	4	5	6	7
Easily Tempted	1	2	3	4	5	6	7
Rational	1	2	3	4	5	6	7
Methodical	1	2	3	4	5	6	7
Enjoy Spending	1	2	3	4	5	6	7
A Planner	1	2	3	4	5	6	7

THANK YOU FOR YOUR TIME!

Lightning Source UK Ltd.
Milton Keynes UK
UKOW02f2207260813

215996UK00011B/1061/P